THE
SASQUATCH
SEEKER'S
FIELD MANUAL

THE
SASQUATCH SEEKER'S
FIELD MANUAL

USING CITIZEN SCIENCE TO UNCOVER NORTH AMERICA'S MOST ELUSIVE CREATURE

DAVID GEORGE GORDON

ILLUSTRATIONS BY
RICHARD L. GOETTLING

MOUNTAINEERS
BOOKS

Mountaineers Books is the publishing division of The Mountaineers, an organization founded in 1906 and dedicated to the exploration, preservation, and enjoyment of outdoor and wilderness areas.

MOUNTAINEERS BOOKS

1001 SW Klickitat Way, Suite 201, Seattle, WA 98134
800.553.4453, www.mountaineersbooks.org

Printed in the United States of America

First edition, 2015

Copyeditor: Anne Moreau
Designer: Jen Grable
Illustrator: Richard L. Goettling
Cartographer: Matt Dressler

Selected hikes in this book were inspired by books in the *Day Hiking* guidebook series (published by Mountaineers Books), by authors Craig Romano, Dan Nelson, and Tami Asars, as well as by US Forest Service and BC Parks information.

Cover illustration by Richard L. Goettling
Frontispiece: An artist's conception of Sasquatch, based on eyewitness reports and footprint casts

Library of Congress Cataloging-in-Publication Data
Gordon, David G. (David George), 1950–
   The Sasquatch seeker's field manual : using citizen science to uncover North America's most elusive creature / David George Gordon ; illustrations by Richard L. Goettling.—First edition.
      pages cm
   Includes bibliographical references and index.
   ISBN 978-1-59485-941-0 (pbk.)—ISBN 978-1-59485-942-7 (ebook)
   1. Sasquatch—North America. 2. Hiking—Equipment and supplies. I. Title.
   QL89.2.S2G674 2015
   001.944—dc23
                                        2014047190

ISBN (paperback): 978-1-59485-941-0
ISBN (ebook): 978-1-59485-942-7

To Karen, a staunch supporter of the Wild Man of the Woods, who understands why we need the Sasquatch more than the Sasquatch needs us, and whom I love with all my heart and soul

"An extraordinary claim requires extraordinary proof."
—Marcello Truzzi

CONTENTS

Part I: Elements of a Successful Sasquatch Search

Part II: Protocols

Part III: Hiking Guide

ACKNOWLEDGMENTS

I wish to thank the many Sasquatch scholars who have generously shared their views, published and unpublished, with me. They include John Bindernagel, Peter Byrne, Loren Coleman, René Dahinden, John Green, Richard Greenwell, Grover Krantz, Jeff Meldrum, Matt Moneymaker, Robert W. Morgan, Kathy Moskowitz Strain, John Napier, Brian Regal, and Wayne Suttles. I also wish to thank my agent, Anne Depue, as well as copyeditor Anne Moreau, editor Laura Shauger, cartographer Matt Dressler, and illustrator Richard Goettling. Three cheers for Jen Grable, production coordinator; Kate Rogers, editor in chief; and Helen Cherullo, publisher, all of Mountaineers Books. I am extremely grateful to my family, friends, and fellow members of the Northwest Science Writers Association for their enthusiastic support of this endeavor.

INTRODUCTION

I'm often asked whether the Sasquatch really exists. In 1992, around the time of the publication of *Field Guide to the Sasquatch*, my initial book on this subject, I'd answer that I was a fence sitter. I would explain that if I said there was no such thing and, shortly thereafter, someone found and photographed the Sasquatch—well, I'd be wrong, wouldn't I? But, I'd also tell people that I wouldn't go to court with the evidence we had collected so far. Basically, I'd tell my interlocutors, I could go either way.

More than two decades have passed since that earlier work was released, and my answer to the question has expanded. Now, when people ask if I think there's something out there—something big and hairy and wild and mysterious—I answer, "I really don't know. You tell me."

So my stance hasn't changed all that much—I'm still divided on the status, real or imagined, of what could very well be the most sensational being on the North American continent. However, my stance on the implications of the question, and how it will be answered, has changed. Now I feel that the responsibility for solving this long-standing mystery rests on the shoulders of all of us: *you*, the readers of this book, and all who work together to discover the truth.

If this riddle is ever answered, it won't, in all probability, happen because some fortunate soul manages to follow this creature's footsteps back to its forested lair. Believe me, many skilled individuals and, in several instances, entire teams of experts, have tried to do just that and have returned with precious little to show for it. Perhaps that's because there's too much unexplored terrain in the Pacific Northwest for one person or group of people to cover. Or maybe the Sasquatch is too evasive for even these experienced individuals to find on their own.

But what if we could combine the efforts of several thousand people trained in reconnaissance, skilled in the techniques of field biology, and equipped with the necessary gear to work on this case? What if we harnessed the power of large groups of people working together to solve problems? I maintain it will take no less than that—thousands of pairs of eyes and ears, collectively gathering and sharing information that can further our understanding and, ultimately, lead us to this mysterious mammal, if indeed that's what it is.

That's where you—and this field manual—come in.

This book is divided into three major sections. The first part lays out the basics about the Sasquatch, offering an overview of what we know so far, the creature's probable basic biology, life history, and place in cultures and belief systems from around the world. Along the way, it also introduces the tenets of citizen science, the rules governing the naming of animals and plants, and the relatively new science of cryptozoology.

The second part of this book contains information on mounting a Sasquatch search. It also explains the standard operating procedures, or protocols, for amassing evidence from fieldwork and sharing it with scientists and other Sasquatch seekers.

The final part includes a selection of suitable locations for day hikes that take you into some of the prime Sasquatch-searching territory in British Columbia, Washington (two areas), Oregon, and California. These five sites were selected because of their significance in Sasquatch lore; they may well be the best places for finding important evidence or even seeing the creature firsthand in the wild. They are areas where people have had close encounters in the past or where a record of Sasquatch sightings exists. I must admit that I also chose these spots for their entertainment value: there's a good yarn connected with each of the sites—which you can use to inspire your hiking companions as they ready themselves for a long and, hopefully, productive day of Sasquatch seeking.

PART

I

ELEMENTS OF A SUCCESSFUL SASQUATCH SEARCH

"There are more things in heaven and earth, Horatio, than are dreamt of in your philosophy." —William Shakespeare, *Hamlet*

THE SUCCESS OF ANY SASQUATCH-SEEKING expedition rests on seeing, hearing, or finding signs of this large but reclusive being. Ultimately, though, an expedition's success will depend on what happens *after* that initial encounter, when the seekers return from the backcountry and start to share their unusual findings with others.

Hearing the news that a large apelike being is lurking in the nearby woods may cause some people to panic (see Interviewing Eyewitnesses in Part II). Others may declare that the entire thing is utter nonsense. Some may even ascribe it to the devil's hand. A fourth group will want to thoroughly examine the evidence before drawing any conclusions. Those people may ask that any information be turned over to the experts— zoologists, anthropologists, criminologists, and so on—for in-depth study.

You *did* bring back evidence, didn't you?

Possibly not. You and your associates may have been so freaked out by your run-in with a wild man of the woods that you didn't think to use your smartphones to capture a video or an audio recording of what you witnessed. After the initial shock wore off, you might have been eager to alert the authorities—so much so that you didn't pause to jot down information about your surroundings. You may have neglected to look for footprints or take measurements of any that you may have found. If there were secondary signs of the Sasquatch's presence, such as swatches of hair or samples of scat, you might not have noticed, or if you did, perhaps you failed to take measures to keep the samples in a safe, secure, and stable environment for later analysis by a laboratory.

When you told your story to the first highway patrol officers or park rangers you could find, they might have taken notes as you tried to explain what you had just seen. When you were finished with your lengthy narrative, they may have written a report, no more than a paragraph or two, summarizing what you just said. They may have added a note, suggesting that what you had seen was actually a brown bear or a black bear. Then they'd go back to work. Days, weeks, or months later, your eyewitness account might appear in the local newspaper or on the nightly news. Eventually, it could wind up as a greatly exaggerated and inaccurate article in one of those sketchy checkout-stand tabloids (see Bigfoot's Baby sidebar, below).

Over the past two decades, I've spoken with dozens of people like this—the ones I call "I-Seen-Ums"—who have had firsthand experiences with Sasquatches while hunting, camping, or simply walking through the countryside. They've told me about a funny smell they noticed or how the hair on the back of their neck stood up, all of a sudden, right before their encounter with the unexplained took place. Some of these I-Seen-Ums have taken me aside and shown me their private collections of casts—

plaster impressions of the enormous footprints they had found in wilderness areas far from humankind. Others have played recordings of what they swore were the Sasquatch's cries, made by audiophiles in the redwoods of California or the rain forests of Vancouver Island, British Columbia. However, none of them could tell me much more than the obvious—what it felt like to be confronted by something big and brutish, something that could possibly be our very closest of kin.

None of them could offer what I consider the important details—things like the time of day when the sighting occurred; what the air temperature may have been; what species of trees, shrubs, and grasses were present; and what the GPS coordinates were. While the episodes were no doubt very significant to those who experienced them, a fact-hungry mind requires specifics. You see, those seemingly insignificant details could help determine when the Sasquatch is most active, the type of habitat it prefers, and what areas its territory encompasses: critical information for determining where to send other Sasquatch seekers on follow-up expeditions. Because of this shortcoming, the I-Seen-Ums' contributions to our understanding of the Sasquatch and its place in our world are bound to be slight.

But what if you had acted otherwise? Let's say you had been specially trained to glean those all-important details about your find. You took concise and reliable field notes; gathered evidence by using established scientific tools and techniques; followed the protocols for safely handling, transporting, and storing said evidence; and carefully catalogued any photos, videos, and audio recordings of the event. Then what?

By doing these things, your information could be studied by others and compared with the similarly well-documented findings of seekers on the Sasquatch's trail. Eventually your evidence could be confirmed by science and the conclusions broadly accepted as fact. Instead of appearing in the tabloids, your accounts might be presented in the *American Journal of Primatology* or any number of other reputable scientific publications. In short, by gathering and presenting those essential details, you could make significant contributions to our knowledge of nature and perhaps answer the question once and for all—does the Sasquatch really exist?

CITIZEN SCIENCE

Our chances of resolving this mystery will be vastly improved if we apply citizen science to the case. Don't feel bad if you haven't heard this term before; the name *citizen science* is a new one, in use for only forty or fifty years. It's a blanket term for projects that involve people outside of con-

BIGFOOT'S BABY

"I HAD BIGFOOT'S BABY" read the banner headline on the *Weekly World News* of September 22, 1992. The accompanying story went on to describe how Katie Martin, a twenty-nine-year-old secretary from Seattle, had an affair with a Bigfoot in July of 1987.

From that relationship, the tabloid alleged, came a "very furry" son. The head and face of Kelly Kendall Martin, the supposed Bigfoot-human hybrid, was covered with curly brown hair, the *Weekly World News* reported. "I could shave his face but he knows that Bigfoot is his daddy and he's proud of that," Kelly's mom was quoted as saying.

As the story explained, Martin came face-to-face with the seven-and-a-half-foot hominid while on a solo camping trip to Mount Rainier National Park. Martin fainted, only to be revived by the Bigfoot, who supposedly dribbled creek water on her face and "tenderly stroked her hair." On subsequent days, he brought Martin flowers, berries, and fresh fish. As time passed, Martin and Bigfoot began communicating telepathically. Returning to her home >>>

ventional scientific circles yet who have been trained to collect reliably accurate information, or data, about nature and the environment. In short, it puts so-called citizen scientists to work on projects that, historically, have been assigned to acknowledged experts in their fields.

It's a new word but hardly a new idea. Two centuries ago, nearly all scientists earned a living by other means. Only in the late 1800s were people fully funded as scientists, typically as employees of industrial laboratories, government-run museums, or academic institutions. As the years passed, these professional scientists and their successors became exclusionary, making it difficult for anyone outside their circles—so-called amateur scientists—to join in. Thanks to citizen science, there are now more opportunities for some of those amateurs to become members of all sorts of scientific research teams.

Of course, the new recruits must learn the language and operating procedures of modern science. To help fulfill this educational need,

---

<<< in Seattle after two weeks, Martin learned she was pregnant with Bigfoot's baby.

The *Seattle Times* ran a follow-up story the same week that issue of the *Weekly World News* hit the stands. One of the *Times'* investigative reporters made a phone call to the sole-listed Kate Martin in the phone book. The call was answered by a man who denied he was Bigfoot and also declined to reveal his true identity. Eventually Martin returned the call, explaining that she was not the mother of Littlefoot nor had she ever been to Mount Rainier. The managing editor of the *Weekly World News* declined to talk about how his paper came by its "world exclusive."

Did Martin believe in Bigfoot's existence? "Heck, I do now," she told the *Seattle Times* reporter.

---

various guidance documents and procedure manuals have been created, field-tested, and adopted by citizen science teams throughout the world. Alas, such guidance materials have not been devised for cryptozoological research. Among this book's many intentions is to provide some preliminary protocols for gathering, reporting, and sharing data about the Sasquatch to fill this void.

FROM FLOWER BUDS TO DEAD BIRDS

Amassing environmental data can be expensive and labor intensive, often involving hundreds of hours of data-gathering activities. Even when equipment needs are negligible, the costs associated with such activities can be high. For example, a fisheries observer aboard a salmon fishing vessel in the Gulf of Alaska might be paid from $200 to $300 per day at sea. To gather a useful data set, the observer might spend six months on one project, bringing the total cost of the fish watcher's services into the $25,000 to $40,000 range. And what about multiyear studies? Now we're talking about $100,000 or more. No wonder more and more financially strapped decision makers are turning to citizen science to get the numbers they need.

It turns out that citizen science is a win-win proposition: People get training in scientifically accepted techniques for collecting, sorting, and, sometimes, analyzing data. In return, they share their insights about observable phenomena—for example, the migratory patterns of wild birds or butterflies, or the waxing and waning of local amphibian populations—natural phenomena that may be happening, quite literally, in their own backyards.

Cornell University in Ithaca, New York, is one of the most active proponents of citizen science. Its Lab of Ornithology manages the activities of an estimated two hundred thousand volunteers of all ages and from all walks of life. Guided by Cornell faculty, technicians, and students, this workforce conducts counts of backyard bird feeders, getting info on the comings and goings of various bird species. It also maps wildlife habitats, measures the parenting successes and failures of nesting birds, and monitors the spread of West Nile virus and other avian diseases. In what may be the largest of citizen science projects, Cornell coordinates numerous seasonal bird counts, in which novice and experienced bird-watchers take to the field to tally the numbers of birds seen during a single day. The lab offers a roster of peer-reviewed publications presenting the findings based on citizen science–collected data—firm evidence of the effectiveness of this grassroots approach.

The nonprofit Conservation Northwest is another worthy citizen-science supporter. Its volunteers set up remote-controlled cameras in Washington State's North Cascades to retrieve images of grizzlies and other imperiled wildlife. Through its programs, also in the North Cascades, the National Park Service gets volunteers outdoors to observe how alpine plants adapt to climate change. Or citizen scientists can take field notes on the North Cascades' resident pika populations, which have been dwindling in recent years. In Oregon, there's Portland Budwatch, a program that focuses on plant phenology, that is, the exact dates and times that buds open in the spring or when leaves start to turn in the fall and how those relate to climate conditions.

There's even a program that trains volunteers to seek out and report the gory details on any dead seabirds found washed ashore on coastal beaches. Headquartered at the University of Washington, the Coastal Observation and Seabird Survey Team (COASST) has grown from a small but devoted group of beach walkers into a cadre of nearly five hundred volunteers. That makes COASST the largest beached-bird network in the world. Initially focused exclusively on Washington shores, it now has operational hubs in Northern California, Oregon, and southeast Alaska.

Upon joining the program, new recruits are given their own bound copy of the COASST protocols for research—where to go, when to go, what to wear, what to look for (beached birds, right?), and how to work alone and with others to contribute meaningful insights to our understanding of the vast and complex Pacific Ocean ecosystem. They're also given a fat, spiral-bound field guide for the sorts of seabird carcasses

CITIZEN SCIENCE IN SPACE

In all fairness, there are people who think that using citizen science in the search for the Sasquatch is a little far out. What, then, would those people think of a citizen science project that gets volunteers to review data from radio telescopes, scanning the universe for signs of extraterrestrial life?

From 2012 to 2014, the SETILive project made data from the Allen Telescope Array (ATA) in Hat Creek, California, available for anyone to see. The project's motive was simple: the more eyes to assess the steady stream of signals from outer space, the better the chances that the significant ones would be identified for further study.

Space is a noisy place and the Allen Telescope Array's automated signal routinely ignores the signals that our planet's communication and entertainment technologies generate. However, signals from distant technologies—ones suggesting the existence of life on planets other than our own—could be hidden within all this noise. Through SETILive, a legion of citizen scientists sifts through the data and, if enough of them see a potential extraterrestrial signal, the ATA is directed to take a closer look at the signal's source.

The project was the brainchild of astronomer Jill Tarter of the SETI Institute, a nonprofit scientific and educational organization with the mission of exploring, understanding, and explaining the origin >>>

they are most likely to come across. Data sheets and other items can be downloaded from the "Volunteer Toolbox" area of the COASST website.

Through the volunteers' combined efforts and the transformation of their individual data into baselines, any impact, human caused or natural in origin, can be assessed. For instance, the effects of a toxic algae bloom—an event that can poison small fish that certain seabirds feed on—can be safely studied hundreds of miles from its point of origin. Likewise, by counting the numbers and kinds of seabirds whose feathers have been fouled by oil, important data can be obtained on unreported oil spills on the open sea. Thanks to citizen science, the damage from such disasters can be assessed, helping to guide any spill containment and cleanup activities.

<<< and nature of life in the universe. It is one of dozens of examples of citizen science projects currently focused on outer space. Opportunities for amateur asteroid hunters, moon-crater counters, and meteor watchers abound. The portal for many of these projects is called Zooniverse; it is owned and operated by the nonprofit Citizen Science Alliance.

In fact, some scientists maintain that the very first citizen science project was born on November 13, 1833, when astronomer Denison Olmsted posted a plea for volunteer meteor shower observers in the New Haven *Daily Herald*. Newspapers nationwide picked up Olmsted's call for help and, soon after, responses came pouring in. Thanks to citizen scientists, Olmsted was able to make a series of groundbreaking observations about the origins of meteor showers.

Now, that's far out.

SCIENTIFIC NOMENCLATURE

If proving the existence of the Sasquatch is an endeavor for citizen scientists, we will need to know the protocols for naming a new species. In the biological sciences, the requirements are straightforward: a well-researched and concisely written description of this creature and an individual, living or dead, that can serve as a reference, or type specimen, to establish beyond a shadow of a doubt what the Sasquatch looks like.

In practice, the path to naming a new species follows these steps: A person must first describe the animal in writing. The description must be published and made accessible to scientists. A preserved specimen of the animal awaiting its name must accompany the description. This preserved specimen, or type, is the example of what a member of this species looks like. The types are extremely valuable to science, so they are usually given to large museums for safekeeping and for others to examine when the need arises.

The rules governing how the new species is named and categorized were first laid out in the 1750s by a Swedish botanist named Carl von Linné. Writing under the pen name of Carolus Linnaeus, he published the *Systema Naturae*—a system for naming animals and plants. His scheme involved assigning names, usually descriptive, to each living or extinct thing. We call this system the binomial or Linnaean system, and it's the system that scientists use today.

The basic unit of the Linnaean system is the *species*, defined as a group of animals or plants that are able to interbreed. A bunch of related species is assigned to a *genus*, the next level up in the classificatory scheme. If you think that two names for one creature is a bit of overkill, consider how your own name is composed: your first name tells us who you are, and the second tells us the family you belong to. The binomial structure of the Linnaean system is just like that, only last name (genus) first.

Genera (that's the plural of *genus*) are bundled together and put into families, the next biggest unit in the Linnaean system. In turn, families are put into orders, which are then placed in classes and phyla (plural for *phylum*). For some groups of plants or animals, additional categories have been created—subgenus, subfamily, superclass, and so on.

To illustrate how this works, let's use our own species, *Homo sapiens*. The first word, *Homo*, is the genus, while the second, *sapiens*, is the species name. There is only one living member of the genus *Homo*. As far as we know, the other members of the genus, *Homo habilis*, *Homo erectus*, *Homo neanderthalensis*, and a bunch of other species, became extinct hundreds of thousands of years ago. The members of the world's human population may look very different, but they can all interbreed. Despite what you might have read in the *Midnight Star*, species cannot interbreed with those in related genera—gorillas, for instance, can't mate successfully with chimpanzees, bonobos, orang-utans, or people.

In Linnaeus's day, determining how genera, families, and orders of animals were interrelated was based on physical resemblances. Did the animals in a taxonomic group have the same number and kinds of teeth? Did they have similar anatomical features or specialized arrangements of body parts (for example, the modified forelimbs of bats or the flippers and tail fins of dolphins and whales)?

Using that kind of logic, people have made plenty of mistakes in naming new species and assigning them to their proper genus, family, or order. For instance, Linnaeus classified the common raccoon as a member of the bear family. This stripe-tailed mammal was eventually reassigned to the suborder Caniformia, the doglike carnivores. Incidentally, the raccoon's scientific name, assigned by Linnaeus in 1758, is *Procyon lotor*. It means "before-dog washer" in Latin.

Likewise, the insect we call the American cockroach, *Periplaneta americana*, was named by Linnaeus from a type specimen he obtained from the New World. How was he to know that this species of cockroach was introduced to the Americas by Spanish galleons carrying slaves from Africa, along with the pest insects of their homeland?

With the advent of genetic testing in the 1980s, the chromosomal makeup of species could now be studied using an extremely fine-toothed comb. As a result, genetic testing dramatically changed the way we view the relationships among the 7.8 million living species that compose the animal kingdom. In many instances, the entire system for classifying certain animals and plants, from genus to order, has been reworked after a review of the genetic evidence.

In the modern era, the International Commission on Zoological Nomenclature (ICZN) has the responsibility for making the final call concerning the legitimacy of all new species. In a year, they may pass judgment on as many as fifteen thousand new animal species, the vast majority of which are recently discovered insects.

But remember, for new animals to be formally recognized, there must be a type specimen for every one of these new species, whether a big mammal or a barely visible gnat—which is why the Sasquatch has yet to receive a scientific name or be recognized by science as a biological entity. That deal-killing detail hasn't prevented some Sasquatch experts from approaching the ICZN, ultimately without success (see the section on Grover Krantz, in Last of an Ancient Lineage?, later in this chapter).

Producing a type specimen does not necessarily require that a Sasquatch be killed. Certainly, there are ethical considerations to taking the life of what could be our next of kin. Uncovering a skull or partial skeleton of a Sasquatch could help pave the road to species-dom. After all, the acceptance of many species of dinosaurs and prehistoric mammals has been based on little more than skeletal remains.

Not only is killing a Sasquatch potentially unethical but in Skamania County, Washington, it's also against the law. In 1969, after a series of Sasquatch sightings were reported, the county's board of commissioners passed an ordinance making the "willful and wanton slaying" of a Sasquatch a felony. Violators of Ordinance No. 69-01 could be punished "by a fine not to exceed $10,000 and/or imprisonment in the county jail for a period not to exceed five years." The county's Sasquatch protection ordinance was amended in 1984, reducing the crime to a gross misdemeanor, punishable by a fine of $1000 and only a single year in jail. If the killing was shown to be "without malice aforethought," the fine was lowered to $500 and six months in jail.

In 2012, Peter Wiemer, founder of the Chautauqua Lake Bigfoot Expo, wrote to New York State's Department of Environmental Conservation, asking them to safeguard the Sasquatch with a no-hunting provision. After some thought, the state declined to take protective measures, responding in a letter to Wiemer "no program or action in relation to a mythical animal is warranted."

THE PRIMATE FAMILY TREE

Is the Sasquatch *that* closely related to humanity as to warrant an ordinance protecting it from injury? From a biologist's perspective, the evidence we've gathered suggests that this individual is most likely a member of the taxonomic order Primates—one of nineteen such groupings of existing and extinct mammals.

The primates share certain physical characteristics. Like all mammals, they are warm-blooded, give birth to live young, and possess paired mammary glands for nursing their offspring. A primate's most distinctive features are its hands and feet. Each of these has five digits. These digits (we call them fingers and toes) are designed for grasping and holding things. One of the digits on each hand is unique—it is shorter and points inward, toward the palm of the hand. You guessed it: it's the thumb.

A primate thumb is what's known as opposable—its system of muscles and tendons give its bearer a tighter, more focused grip. Evolutionary biologists believe the opposable thumb was of great benefit to the earliest humans, allowing them to make and use primitive tools. It turns out that tool making and use is not restricted to our kind: there have been several fairly recent discoveries of gorillas and chimpanzees shaping twigs into "fish hooks" to snag edible termites. A group of bonobos in the Congo is

DE LOYS'S APE

In 1920, a Swiss team of geological surveyors was looking for petroleum in the jungles of Colombia. Led by Dr. François de Loys, the team had been at it for three years. Throughout their exploratory mission, they suffered an assortment of tropical diseases and endured the occasional hostilities of the region's indigenous tribes.

One day, the team was startled by two apelike figures coming their way. These creatures walked upright, were about five feet tall, and, unlike all other known species of New World primate, appeared to be lacking tails. One was thought to be a male and the other a female. Seeing the geologists, the hominid pair started to behave aggressively. They tore up the ground and, in a manner not unlike chimpanzees and baboons at zoos, began to throw their feces at the geologists. As the "apes" advanced, making further threats, the geologists reached for their rifles and opened fire, killing the female and wounding the male, which ran bleeding into the forest.

De Loys and the men examined the carcass, counted its teeth, and took some photos. Then, they chopped up the body and gave the head to the expedition's cook, who is said to have boiled it and later used the cranium as a salt-storage vessel. All but one of the photographs was swept away by a flash flood or (depending on `>>>`

known to make walking staffs from tree branches and use them to gauge the depths of the water in potentially fordable streams.

Tool use is one of several adaptations that allowed the primates to swing to the top of the evolutionary tree. They have exceptionally large brains (expressed as a ratio of brain size to body mass) that can process environmental information and make swift decisions when the need arises. Another prize-winning primate characteristic is forward-facing eyes. These give the animal a stereoscopic view of any friends, foes, and food in the vicinity.

Scientists have divided the order Primates into two suborders. The pro-simians (informally known as "almost monkeys") include lemurs, lorises,

<<< which version of the story you read) was lost when the team's boat capsized.

Returning to Europe, Dr. de Loys and an associate wrote a suite of scientific papers on their find. Based on the measurements they took and the animal's dental records—it had four fewer teeth than any other species of New World primate—the two proposed that a scientific name, *Ameranthropoides loysi* or "de Loys's apelike American," be given to this critter. The scientific community declined to honor their request.

According to Ivan Sanderson, the subject of de Loys's photo was most likely a spider monkey (genus *Ateles*) with its tail lopped off. Seated on a small wooden crate, with a stick propping up its chin, the mutilated corpse of the monkey was made to look much larger, about five feet tall, in keeping with de Loys's fictitious claim. "The original photograph is not just a case of mistaken identity; it is an outright hoax, and an obnoxious one at that, being a deliberate deception," Sanderson fumed in *Abominable Snowmen: Legend Come to Life.*

and tarsiers—fairly small, nocturnally active tree-dwellers of Southeast Asia, Africa, and Madagascar. They have large eyes, many have long fingers, and a few have venomous bites. Primatologists believe that the prosimians represent the earliest evolutionary stages of primate life. An ancient tale from the Philippines tells us that tarsiers are pets belonging to the spirits that live in giant fig trees. Frighten or harm a tarsier and you better apologize to the spirits, the story goes.

The second suborder of Primates is the anthropoids, also known as the simians. These are the so-called higher primates: New World monkeys, Old World monkeys, apes and—saving the best for last—people. Unlike the prosimians, anthropoid primates are active by day and tend to spend more time on the ground than up in the trees. Overall, anthropoids are bigger and bulkier than their prosimian kin. The world's largest primate is the eastern lowland gorilla (*Gorilla beringei graueri*), an anthropoid ape that can weigh more than 450 pounds. Next to that, the smallest, Berthe's mouse lemur (*Microcebus berthae*), looks like lunch meat. When fully grown, it weighs the same as a first-class letter—about an ounce.

Scientists further divide the anthropoid primates into nine families. The family that appears most relevant to the search for the Sasquatch is the apes—a grouping of twenty-four species of tailless primates, all of whom have exceptionally well developed limbs for getting around in the treetops. Siamangs and gibbons from Southeast Asia and China use their muscular five-foot-long arms to launch themselves, and, with a series of twenty-foot leaps, they can traipse through the tropical rain forest, making parallel bars and trapezes out of its lattice of vines and tree limbs. These natural acrobats are also fairly accomplished at walking erect, holding those long and lithe arms as counterweights to help keep their balance.

For their part, orangutans lead mostly arboreal lives, infrequently leaving their nests in tall trees to venture onto the forest floor. These are big guys, too. Adult male orangutans can be nearly six feet tall and weigh more than 260 pounds. Two species are currently recognized by science: the Sumatran orangutan (*Pongo abelii*) and the Bornean orangutan (*Pongo pygmaeus*). On a cryptozoological note, the name for this animal, *orang-utan*, means "man of the forest" in the Malay and Indonesian languages.

Chimpanzees and their close cousins, bonobos, spend relatively more time on the ground than do the aforementioned siamangs, gibbons, and orangs. However, they do not really walk erect by our standards. In the entire animal kingdom, only humankind appears to have received the gift of erect posture—admittedly, a costly gift, judging by the number of chiropractors, massage therapists, and back specialists with thriving practices. Because chimpanzees and bonobos move with their weight distributed among all four limbs, a mode of self-transport known as knuckle-walking works best.

This is not to say that chimps can't stand on their hind legs. They will rise up and walk forward or back with what might look to us like the rubber-legged gait of a sailor on shore leave. Nonetheless, these moments of erectitude are the exception, not the rule.

The two species of gorilla, the western and the eastern, make quantum leaps upward in terms of size. Standing upright, a mature male might be more than five foot eight and weigh as much as 350 pounds. (The tallest gorilla on record, by the way, was a six-foot-three-inch individual shot by a hunter in what is now the Democratic Republic of the Congo, seventy-some years ago.)

Like the other great apes, gorillas are knuckle-walkers. Sure, they can pull themselves into an upward stance—we've all seen those chest-thumping scenes on TV documentaries—but, when not sitting or lying down, gorillas spend most of their time on all fours. Reclusive by nature, adults and their young spend most of their days eating, playing, napping, and building day beds and night nests out of the leaves and limbs of the dense underbrush. They will take to the trees to feed on fruit, nuts, and foliage or to

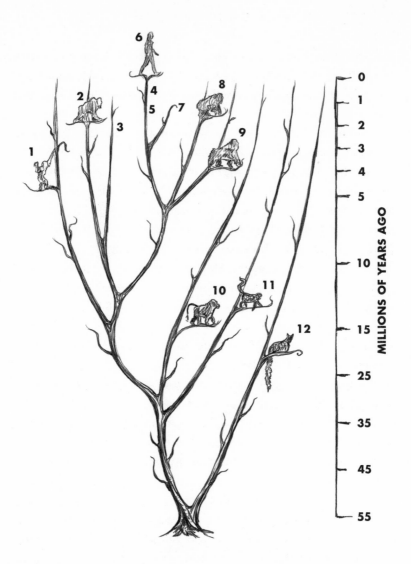

Figure 1. A hypothetical family tree for the Primates: 1. gibbons, 2. orangutans, 3. Gigantopithecines, 4. *Homo sapiens neanderthalensis*, 5. *Homo erectus*, 6. modern humans, 7. *Australopithecus robustus*, 8. chimpanzees, 9. gorillas, 10. Old World monkeys, 11. New World monkeys, and 12. lemurs

escape from predators and, sometimes, from other gorillas laying claim to their turf. It makes more sense, anatomically speaking, for gorillas to carry their apish physiques like most other mammals, relying on two pair, not one pair, of limbs.

Before we rule out the great apes as possible Sasquatch kin, let's briefly entertain the notion that our mysterious primate is a species heretofore unknown. What's the likelihood of that, you may ask? Well, consider this: Until 2007, scientists weren't aware of the lesula (*Cercopithecus lomamiensis*), a new species of Old World monkey. They discovered the first one, a juvenile female, in the home of a primary school director in the Democratic Republic of the Congo. Likewise, the bonobo wasn't granted species status until 1933.

Still, this knuckle-walking business is perplexing. To the ill informed, it might seem that no kind of primate truly walks erect—that is, other than ourselves.

A PORTRAIT OF THE SASQUATCH

With the goal of meeting the scientific requirements for naming a new species in mind, let's take a look at what we know about the Sasquatch, starting with a generalized profile of this enigmatic being. My favorite description of the Sasquatch appears in the *Washington Environmental Atlas*, a 114-page black pleather-bound folio, produced in 1975 by the Seattle District of the US Army Corps of Engineers, with help from the University of Washington's Institute for Environmental Studies. This authoritative document contains information about the geological features, archeological sites, ponds, lakes and rivers, forests, plants, and animals of the Evergreen State. On page 53, opposite a spread on native reptiles and amphibians, is this definition of the Sasquatch:

> *Information from alleged sightings, tracks, and other experiences conjures up the picture of an apelike creature standing between*

eight and 12 feet tall, weighing in excess of 1000 pounds, and tak-
ing strides of up to six feet. Plaster casts have been made of tracks
showing a large, squarish foot, 14 to 24 inches in length and 5 to 10
inches in breadth. Reported to feed on vegetation and some meat,
the Sasquatch is covered with long hair, except for the face and
hands, and has a distinctly humanlike form.

Short, sweet, and unquestionably guarded in tone, the *Washington Environmental Atlas*'s entry continues to summarize all that was known about Sasquatch at the time. It is agile, the entry tells us, with great strength and endurance to cover an extensive range in search of food, shelter, and others of its kind. This creature is also quite shy and leaves minimal evidence—primarily footprints—to establish its presence.

The atlas's entry concludes with an indirect call to arms: "If Sasquatch is purely legendary, the legend is likely a long time in dying. On the other hand, if Sasquatch does exist, then with the Sasquatch hunts being mounted and the increasing human population it seems likely that some hard evidence may soon be in hand. Legendary or actual, Sasquatch excites a great popular interest in Washington."

The optimistic claim—that "hard evidence may soon be in hand"— was made four decades ago. In that time, Washington's human population has nearly doubled. Hundreds of thousands of acres of prime Sasquatch habitat have been cleared, graded, and turned into subdivisions, shopping malls, industrial parks, and private estates. And a number of large-scale Sasquatch searches have been mounted, oftentimes at great expense. Contrary to the Army Corps of Engineers' expectations, very little information has been acquired with which to flesh out their forty-year-old species profile.

What we *have* gathered over all this time is an extensive collection of reported Sasquatch sightings. The online database of the Bigfoot Field

Researchers Organization (BFRO), which incidentally bills itself as "the only scientific research organization exploring the Bigfoot/Sasquatch mystery," contains nearly fourteen hundred reports of Sasquatch activity in Washington, Oregon, California, and British Columbia. That's more than three times the total number of sightings and footprint discoveries from these same states and province before the Army Corps of Engineers' environmental atlas was published. Some of the reports on both the environmental atlas and the BFRO database are archaic, originally filed in the 1920s and 1930s. However, the majority are from more recent decades. The BFRO website is updated frequently, with postings of fresh sightings and footprint finds within days of their occurrence.

As with statistics about shark attacks, the volume of data and anecdotes amassed on the Sasquatch rises and falls periodically, in part due to the level of public interest in the subject. Sasquatch scholars such as Loren Coleman, author of *Mysterious America* and several other books on the unexplained, see a progression of events, beginning with the stories of the legendary Abominable Snowmen told by climbers of Mount Everest in the 1950s and leading up to the Sasquatch phenomenon of today.

These early accounts may have inspired others to go public about their experiences with similar apelike beings in California and the northwestern states. Coleman discovered that interest in the Sasquatch reached a peak in the late 1960s and early 1970s, following the release of what is now referred to as the Patterson-Gimlin film—a brief 16-millimeter movie of a female Bigfoot walking briskly away from the camera in the Bluff Creek watershed in Northern California.

Looking for a link here? One of the filmmakers, Roger Patterson of Yakima, Washington, had written and illustrated a book, *Do Abominable Snowmen of North America Really Exist?*, a year before the movie was taken. Critics of the film cite Patterson's unabashed enthusiasm for the book's subject matter (evidenced in chapter titles such as "Abominable Snowmen Are Here!") as a reason to suspect that Patterson may have been a hoaxster. The text of that now hard-to-find book is available in another Patterson book, *The Bigfoot Film Controversy*, which also includes supplementary material such as newspaper clippings and information on the filming and controversy surrounding it.

Public interest in Bigfoot and the Sasquatch continued to grow steadily, reaching a pinnacle in the late 1990s, according to Coleman, with the emergence of a global internet community. Sensationalistic TV shows such as *In Search Of . . .* or *Unsolved Mysteries* certainly played a role, he says. So did major motion pictures like *Harry and the Hendersons* and, most recently, *Finding Bigfoot*, a prime-time reality TV program on Animal Planet featuring Matt Moneymaker, founder of the BFRO, as one of the show's four expedition leaders. "But it wasn't until the emergence of Sasquatch-themed websites, where people publish field reports and post videos of the creature in question, that things really took off," Coleman informed me in a recent interview. A lot of those websites host symposia and conferences for both novice and experienced Sasquatch seekers.

Coleman predicts that the next phase of public involvement will involve what he calls "cryptotourism"—activities based on the search for unexplained animals such as Sasquatch. "Most people know that these TV shows are bogus," he suggests. "Still, these shows titillate their imaginations. They give people an excuse to wear night vision goggles, and they give them a reason to mount their own Sasquatch outings to sites like the ones they've just seen on *Finding Bigfoot*."

Coleman himself could very well reap the benefits of this surge in interest—as the curator of the International Cryptozoology Museum in Portland, Maine, *and* as the author of *Bigfoot! The True Story of Apes in America*, wherein he reveals the top places in America to see a Sasquatch-like being. It's no surprise that six out of twenty of these hot spots happen to be in the Northwest. "The sightings are so routine in some communities that many recognize their good fortune through road signs, memorials, statues, museums, and gift shops," he writes. Destination travel at its best.

THE SASQUATCH IN BRIEF

Some people claim that the Sasquatch is an alien explorer, parking its spaceship on our planet to take a hike through the Northwest's must-see rain forests. Others insist that Sasquatch is no less than a time traveler, passing through a cosmic wormhole that connects our world to that of prehistory or the future. Still others say that the Sasquatch and a few more-otherworldly animals are from other dimensions, briefly appearing and, then, disappearing into the vapors at will.

Any of these assertions warrant some consideration. Truth be told, they could explain why we've uncovered so little corporeal evidence with which to establish the Sasquatch's legitimacy. However, there is even less evidence to support these creative explanations. Without further proof, phenomena such as intergalactic visitations, time travel, and multidimensional games of hide-and-seek should be regarded as pure speculation—science fiction perhaps, but not science fact. As such, these theories explaining the Sasquatch's elusive nature will be set aside for now as we look for firm proof of a permanent, albeit well-concealed, resident of planet Earth.

People looking for commonalities among those fourteen-hundred-plus reports of brushes with Sasquatches from Northern California north through British Columbia are likely to be disappointed. Beauty may be in the eye of the beholder, and apparently, the Sasquatch is, too. Estimates by eyewitnesses of the Sasquatch's height and weight have been all over the map—from four feet to fourteen feet tall and 400 to 2500 pounds. The color of the Sasquatch's hair is also up for grabs. Although the majority of observers characterize its color as auburn or black, many others have described it as beige or white. Some have said it has a silvery sheen.

Big or small, Sasquatches are often described as apish or monkeylike. Their arms may be long and limber, according to some. They are commonly portrayed as large slope-shouldered hulks—usually lacking any vestige of a neck. It's thought that smaller specimens are females or youngsters and the largest ones are males.

Some reports speak of the Sasquatch's round, reflective eyes—a characteristic usually associated with animals such as owls or aye-ayes that are active by night or during the hours of dawn or dusk. Some people say that Sasquatches give off an extremely foul odor, while others make no mention of this in their reports. Some have heard strange cries, long sonorous whoops, or the sound of someone thumping mightily on the trunk of a tree. Several recordings of what are said to be Sasquatch vocalizations exist, although their authenticity has not been universally agreed upon.

Details about the scene of a human-Sasquatch encounter have also been highly variable. Although the majority of these experiences have taken place in wooded locales, there have also been an abundance of sightings on arid plains and the boulder-strewn slopes of the Cascade Range and Olympic Mountains. And not all of the evidence has been recovered from untrammeled wildlands. The exceptionally large footprints of the Sasquatch have been discovered in farm fields and in recently urbanized areas, too. An example of this latter kind is two sets of tracks uncovered in a newly completed subdivision in Bellevue, Washington, in the 1980s. Analysis of the footprints showed that the tracks' makers had strolled across the recently modified terrain, stopping to peer into the windows of homes on both sides of the street.

Reports of large humanlike beings have been filed in nearly every state and province of North America. However, about a third of them are centered in the Pacific Northwest. In few instances are the people involved able to get a well-lit, unobstructed view of a Sasquatch. More often, a "sighting" involves hearing, smelling, or simply sensing the Sasquatch's presence.

What Sasquatches eat or how they obtain their food is also unclear. Some reports suggest these beings are omnivorous, thriving on a diet that could include berries, nuts, leaves, roots, and fungi as well as salmon, small mammals, and even larger mammals, such as elk or deer. Whether Sasquatches are active hunters or passive scavengers feeding on the carcasses of deer and other big game has not been determined.

The bulk of the physical evidence of the Sasquatch's existence is composed of tracks—that is, footprint impressions left in sand, soft soil, snow, or mud. Thousands of these have been found and documented through photos or filled with casting material to create replicas of the feet that made them. Some of these casts show remarkable detail, with intricately distributed dermatoglyphic patterns—skin patterns that are the equivalent of our fingerprints—that can puzzle even a professional fingerprint expert. In *Field Guide to the Sasquatch*, I wrote about how one of these experts, a man named Doug Monsoor of the Lakewood, Colorado, police department looked at the casts of large footprints from the Umatilla National Forest near Walla Walla, Washington. He was awestruck by the detailed derma ridges—subtle ridges that give texture to toe prints and fingerprints. He concluded that the "sizes, distributions, and orientations of the ridge patterns are consistent with those found on the human foot. . . . If hoaxing were involved, I can conceive of no way in which it could have been done. They appear to be casts of original impressions of a primate foot—of a creature different from any of which I am aware."

Handprints have also been found on occasion. However, the most astounding find in recent years is that of a partial body imprint, located in September 2000 by members of a BFRO research team. At the scene of their discovery, the Skookum Meadows of the Gifford Pinchot National Forest in Washington, the group had left bait such as apples, melons, and other fruit. The team also played audiotapes of purported Sasquatch calls, as well as sounds of crying (human) babies and children at play, in an attempt to lure any hominids from the forests fringing the meadow.

While checking the fruit traps, team members noticed an odd indentation at the edge of a large mud puddle. Analysis of this large impression suggested that a Sasquatch had pressed its body into the mud, possibly in an attempt to retrieve some of the fruit. Apparently, the Sasquatch had sat at the edge of the puddle, leaned forward, and while supporting its bulk with its left forearm, extended its right arm to nab the fruit.

Why had this being gone to such lengths to avoid leaving footprints in the mud? The team reasoned that this Sasquatch was being stealthy, taking measures to avoid leaving any telltale tracks. "If these animals have been avoiding confrontations with humans for thousands of years, might this behavior—avoidance of leaving distinctive footprints—be an ancient

SASQUATCH, DOG, OR GUY IN A SUIT?

Is Chewbacca, the now-familiar character in the original *Star Wars* film trilogy, supposed to be a Sasquatch?

Probably not. Despite the Wookiee's height and hirsute appearance, the character of Chewbacca, Han Solo's first mate, was actually inspired by director George Lucas's Alaskan malamute, Indiana, who would often ride around in the passenger seat of his master's car. In fact, *Star Wars* scholars point out that the name Chewbacca is suspiciously similar to the word собака (sobaka)—Russian for "small dog."

>>>

<<<   The part of "Chewie" (as Han Solo nicknamed him) was played by Peter Mayhew, a seven-foot-three-inch-tall Brit, who, as a youngster, suffered from a genetic affliction known as Marfan syndrome. Now in his 70s, Mayhew wears a size 15½ shoe. The fuzzy boots for the Chewbacca costume were even larger, about a size 16½—a tad under thirteen and a half inches long. That's bigger than the shoes worn by some of the world's tallest basketball players: Wilt Chamberlain (who at the peak of his game was seven feet one inch tall) wore a size 15 athletic shoe, while Kareem Abdul-Jabbar (nearly seven feet two inches tall today) wears a size 16.

While we're on the subject, Robert Wadlow, billed as the World's Tallest Man by Ripley's Believe It or Not! was eight feet eleven inches tall, had an arm span of nine and a half feet, and wore size 37AA shoes, about eighteen and a half inches in length. The International Shoe Company of St. Louis, Missouri, provided his hundred-dollar-a-pair leather lace-ups gratis.

But back to Chewbacca. The costume used in all three of the initial *Star Wars* episodes was built by makeup artist and creature-effects supervisor Stuart Freeborn and designer John Mollo. Freeborn's makeup for Chewbacca was intended to give this citizen of the planet Kashyyyk the look of a cat crossed with a dog.

"I think one of the most fascinating elements of the character is that it is essentially a guy in a monkey suit," Brandon Alinger of the Prop Store, arguably the nation's most extensive trove of movie memorabilia, wrote me in an email. "Yet audiences never really question the believability or lifelikeness of this character," Alinger noted. "He just works."

The original Chewbacca suit—or multiple suits, as it were—is currently in the archives of Lucas's Skywalker Ranch and will soon be on display at a planned Lucas Museum of Narrative Art in Chicago.

survival strategy?" the BFRO incident report asked. The report goes on to suggest that the Sasquatch's use of evasive tactics may be more common than we think, perhaps explaining why we don't find even more obvious signs that a Sasquatch walked here.

NATIVE AMERICAN TESTIMONY

The First Peoples of North America have lived here for many thousands of years. Their lifestyles and belief systems have kept them in close contact with the forces of nature. Over the centuries, they became experts on the rocks, plants, and animals of the regions over which they held provenance. It's no wonder, then, that their relationships with the wild men, some of them unsettlingly similar to what we now call the Sasquatch, were complex.

The name "Sasquatch" is an Anglicized version of the word *Saskehavis*, used by the Chehalis Indian Band (Sts'ailes) of British Columbia's Fraser River Valley. Credit for this name's popularization goes to John W. Burns, a Canadian schoolteacher turned journalist, who wrote about the topic in the 1920s. Burns spent a number of years on the Chehalis Indian Reserve, about sixty miles east of Vancouver, collecting Native tales, many of them describing their run-ins with the Sasquatch. The tales were incorporated into a series of articles published in various Vancouver newspapers.

Burns's most widely read piece was published in the April 1, 1929, issue of *MacLean's*, Canada's national magazine. Titled "Introducing B.C.'s Hairy Giants: A Collection of Strange Tales about British Columbia's Wild Men as Told by Those Who Say They Have Seen Them," the article caused a stir among *MacLean's* readers (see the Charley Victor's Story sidebar, below). In the process, it all but institutionalized the name Sasquatch.

Sasquatch, Seatco, Tsiatko, Skookum, and Boqs

The Chehalis are but one of dozens of tribes whose cosmologies include Sasquatch-like beings. In the book *Giants, Cannibals & Monsters*, anthro-

TRIBAL NAMES FOR SASQUATCH-LIKE HOMINIDS

Saskehavis (Wild Man)..Chehalis

Saskets (Giant) ....Salishan and Sahaptin

Sc'wen 'ey 'til (Tall Burnt Hair)..Spokane

Seatco (Stick Indian) ....Yakima, Klickitas, and Puyallup

See'atco (One Who Runs and Hides) ....Coast Salish

Sesquac or Saskehavas (Wild Man of the Woods) ....Coast Salish

Qelqelitl (Female Sesquac) ....Coast Salish

Skookum (Evil God of the Woods or Mountain Devil) ....Chinook

Source: *Giants, Cannibals & Monsters: Bigfoot in Native Culture*, Kathy Moskowitz Strain, Hancock House, 2008.

pologist Kathy Moskowitz Strain offers an appendix of more than 140 names for unusual beings, some large, some small, but all extraordinarily wild and frightening to the First Peoples. This list draws from the collective wisdom of tribes in all regions of the continent, from central Mexico to the northernmost subarctic and arctic zones of the United States and Canada.

Many of the stories in the book are unquestionably about the Sasquatch or something like him. Others are, well, something else. For example, there's the Cherokee story "The Snake with the Big Feet," which tells how a snake with unusual anatomical attributes is transformed into a human and marries the chief's daughter. Moskowitz Strain explains this latter collection of tales this way: "Clearly, snakes do not have feet; nor do they turn human and marry human females. This story is included because after careful analysis of Cherokee stories, I believe the snake 'represents' a Bigfoot [Sasquatch] (as denoted by the big feet) and the story is designed to help the reader accept that a Bigfoot 'married' a human female."

It's not uncommon, says Moskowitz Strain, for Native American storytellers to alter or hide the true subject of a tale—a device that lets them gradually introduce so-called taboo topics like the Sasquatch in nonthreatening ways. According to Moskowitz Strain, this method may involve taking traits of other animals or humans and bestowing them on the taboo characters in a tale. As a result, there are many Sasquatch-like characters in Native American lore that talk, have homes, and can perform other tasks associated exclusively with people.

But what about the many stories pertaining to recognizable Sasquatch-like beings? Do the tellers of these stories know something that we haven't been privy to, at least not of late? Take this description by James Wickersham, from the October 1898 issue of *Overland Monthly* : "The Seatco is a malicious demon having the form of an Indian, but larger, quick, and stealthy. He inhabits the dark recesses of the woods, where his campfires are often seen; he sleeps by day but sallies forth at dusk for 'a night of it.' He robs traps, breaks canoes, steals food and other portable property; he waylays the belated traveler, and it is said to kill all those whose bodies are found dead. To his wicked and malicious cunning is credited all the unfortunate and malicious acts which cannot otherwise be explained."

Or consider this description of Tsiatko, nemesis of the Puyallup and Nisqually tribes of central and southern Puget Sound. To quote the *Dictionary of the Chinook Jargon, or, Trade Language of Oregon* by George Gibbs, an American geologist and ethnologist in the 1850s:

By some, the Tsiatko are described as of gigantic size, their feet 18 inches long, and shaped like a bear's. They wore no clothes but the body is covered with hair like that of a dog, only not so thick . . . They are said to live in the mountains, in holes underground, and to smell bad. They come down chiefly in the fishing season, at which time the Indians are excessively afraid of them . . . Their voices are like that of an owl, and they possess the power of charming, so that those hearing them become demented or fall down in a swoon.

CHARLEY VICTOR'S STORY

In 1929, J. W. Burns interviewed Charley Victor for his article "Introducing B.C.'s Hairy Giants: A Collection of Strange Tales about British Columbia's Wild Men as Told by Those Who Say They Have Seen Them," published on April 1 of that year in *MacLean's*.

Charley Victor belongs to the Skwah Reserve near Chilliwack. In his younger days he was known as one of the best hunters in the province and had many thrilling adventures in his time.

Did he know anything about the hairy apelike men who were supposed to inhabit the distant mountains? Charley smiled, and answered that he had had a slight acquaintance with them. He had been in what he thought was one of their houses. "And that is not all," said he. "I met and spoke to one of their women, and I shot . . ." But let Charley tell the story himself.

>>>

<<<

"The strange people, of whom there are but few now—rarely seen and seldom met," said the old hunter, "are known by the name of Sasquatch, or, 'the hairy mountain men.'

"The first time I came to know about these people," continued the old man, "I did not see anybody. Three young men and myself were picking salmonberries on a rocky mountain slope some five or six miles from the old town of Yale. In our search for berries we suddenly stumbled upon a large opening in the side of the mountain. This discovery greatly surprised all of us, for we knew every foot of the mountain, and never knew nor heard there was a cave in the vicinity.

"Outside the mouth of the cave there was an enormous boulder. We peered into the cavity but couldn't see anything.

"We gathered some pitchwood, lighted it and began to explore. But before we got very far from the entrance of the cave, we came upon a sort of stone house or enclosure: it was a crude affair. We couldn't make a thorough examination, for our pitchwood kept going out. We left, intending to return in a couple of days and go on exploring. Old Indians, to whom we told the story of our discovery, warned us not to venture near the cave again, as it was surely occupied by the Sasquatch. That was the first time I heard about the hairy men that inhabit the mountains. We, however, disregarded the advice of the old men and sneaked off to explore the cave, but to our great disappointment found the boulder rolled back into its mouth and fitting it so nicely that you might suppose it had been made for that purpose."

>>>

<<<

Charley intimated that he hoped to have enough money some day to buy sufficient dynamite to blow open the cave of the Sasquatch, and see how far it extends through the mountain.

The Indian then took up the thread of his story and told of his first meeting with one of these men. A number of other Indians and himself were bathing in a small lake near Yale. He was dressing, when suddenly out from behind a rock, only a few feet away, stepped a nude hairy man. "Oh! He was a big, big man!" continued the old hunter. "He looked at me for a moment, his eyes were so kind-looking that I was about to speak to him, when he turned about and walked into the forest."

At the same place two weeks later, Charley, together with several of his companions, saw the giant, but this time he ran toward the mountain. This was twenty years after the discovery of the cave.

Equally haunting is the portrayal of the Skookum, a name, presumably for the same being, used by both the Clackamas tribe of northern Oregon and the Chinook tribe living along the lower and middle Columbia River. The Clackamas say that adolescent Skookums must undergo an initiation rite: to become an adult member of their tribe, adolescents must jump in front of a human on the trail and wave their hands in front of the human's face, without being seen.

The Boqs, or "Bush Man," is a familiar figure to the Bella Coola people of British Columbia's central coast. According to the Bella Coola Indians by anthropologist T. F. McIlwraith of the University of Toronto, the Boqs resembles a man—its hands in particular and the region around the eyes.

"It walks on its hind legs, in a stooping posture, its long arms swinging below the knees . . . The entire body, except the face, is covered with long hair, the growth being most profuse on the chest, which is large, corresponding to the great strength of the animal."

Sound like you-know-who? Maybe, but maybe not. The height of McIlwraith's Boqs is "rather less than the average man."

A Study by Suttles

Seatco, Saskets, Boqs. Are these names the monikers of several different kinds of humanlike creatures? Or are they nicknames, if you will, for the same gnarly beast—the one we are currently calling the Sasquatch?

Portland State University professor Wayne Suttles tackled this question in an article written for the spring 1972 issue of *Northwest Anthropological Research Notes*. He examined the various beliefs in what he called "nonhuman primates" among Coast Salish tribes throughout southwestern British Columbia and northeastern Washington. He created a marvelous graph of the commonly reported traits of these nonhumans, broken down by tribal affiliation. All of these creatures, real or imagined, "are giants," Suttles explained, "human in form but bigger than ordinary human beings."

All of these giants make their homes in the woods, according to Suttles. But beyond those attributes, no two types of nonhumans shared the same set of traits. Therefore, Suttles concluded, "most if not all of the Coast Salish of this area seem to agree that there are large, manlike beings in the woods and mountains who differ from human beings in various ways."

Suttles then asked why the Coast Salish people share the traditional belief of giants in the mountains. He came up with six possible explanations, the first one being the most obvious to cryptozoologists: that there might very well be a real creature out there. A second explanation, the anthropologist posited, was that the descriptions were veiled allusions to hostile members of other tribes. As participants in raiding parties, mem-

bers of various tribes probably engaged in kidnapping, wife stealing, mur-
der, and other "war crimes," and these activities may have been attributed
to various Sasquatch-like beings.

The next reason? Believing in mountain-dwelling giants could explain
away rockslides, falling trees, eerie noises, and other natural phenomena.
And there's the possibility that a belief in such monstrous creatures might
affect behaviors in positive ways. In Suttles's words, "Possibly if there are
real people in the mountains who may steal women and children, there is
survival value in imagining that they have super-human proportions and
powers."

THE BOGEYMAN

Gee, I'm scared. Gee, I'm scared
And I don't know what to do.
I just saw a man with a great big hand
And he looks like Boogaboo.
I don't like when it's dark at night.
That's when the bogeyman comes.
If we lay still in bed,
Maybe he'll think we are dead.
Gee, I'm scared. Ain't you?

—Traditional children's song

It's easy to see how parents might use stories of child-eating monsters
to keep their kids a little closer to the campfire and to discourage them
from straying into the woods at night. Indeed, European storytelling tra-
ditions are rife with such cautionary tales about strange characters—the

wicked witch in "Hansel and Gretel" and the cunning, carnivorous wolf in "Little Red Riding Hood." Perhaps the most Sasquatch-like, of these, the boogeyman, or bogeyman, can be traced back to the early twelfth century. It appears as a masculine entity, a female figure, or an androgynous form in numerous children's nursery rhymes and bedtime stories, keeping wayward children on the straight and narrow path, at least for their first few years of life.

That could easily explain the prevalence of cannibals and child-stealing crones throughout Native American lore. The best known of these is Dzunukwa (also spelled Dsonoqua or Tsonoqua). Familiar to the members of the Kwakiutl of northern Vancouver Island, British Columbia, this ominous character is said to have bedraggled black hair, pendulous breasts, heavy eyebrows, and deep-set eyes. Kwakiutl children are told that the sound of the wind blowing through the cedar trees is actually the call of Dzunukwa, pursing her lips and making her characteristic "ooh-ooh, ooh-ooh" call. Even worse, it's said she attracts children by imitating their grandmother's voices.

Of all of Suttles's explanations for the profusion of Sasquatch stories among Northwest tribes, the final two are personal favorites. One suggests that to define ourselves as separate from nature, we need a nonhuman counterpart with which to compare and contrast our more refined selves. The other makes the case that tales of the Sasquatch are just plain fun.

The concept of the "refined" being versus the "unrefined" one is widespread, shared by seemingly disparate groups of people worldwide. It's as if we're all saying, "Hey, you think *we're* bad? Check out these guys over here." In classical Indonesian dance and puppetry, for example, the heroes and heroines are depicted as stately, lithe, and golden-skinned, with small noses and pleasantly streamlined features. In contrast, the villains in these palace art pieces are portrayed as stout and stocky oafs with red skin, bulging eyes, and bulbous noses. Some say these unflattering traits were intended to mimic those of the early Dutch colonists, who were held in contempt by the native Indonesians.

The dichotomy of rough versus refined also appears in the Bible. In the book of Genesis, Esau, the elder twin brother of Jacob, is said to be a "hairy man," while his sibling is "a smooth man." At the urging of his mother, Jacob wears the hides of goat kids on his hands and the back of his neck to deceive his nearly blind father into thinking that he is the hirsute twin. "And he did not recognize him because his hands were hairy like the hands of his brother Esau, and he blessed him," the Bible relates. For some reason, many Bible scholars consider this premeditated deceit—the triumph of the refined over the unrefined—to be fair play.

Suttles's sixth reason for tribal beliefs in Sasquatch is a bit of a surprise, considering the gravity of the others leading up to it: people enjoy the idea of scary things. You need look no farther than the local multiplex movie marquee for proof of that. "There seems to be plenty of evidence around that people enjoy talking about scary things and appreciate a well-told story about a frightening experience," Suttles's *Northwest Anthropological Research Notes* article concludes.

Oral Traditions, Facts, and Fables

The First People did not have written languages. Instead, they relied on oral tradition, keeping their cultures alive by telling and retelling information about their tribes, their surroundings, family lineages, and so on. Although much of this information has been recorded, and is still being recorded by anthropologists and linguists today, a considerable amount has been lost to time, carried to the grave with some tribes' few remaining Native speakers.

The act of transcribing Native stories into English prose is bound to carry with it some cultural baggage. For the transcriber, it's easy to make mistakes—little slipups and big gaffs—while trying to explain broad concepts such as Spirit or the beyond within the much narrower confines of our societal mores.

Attempts to Anglicize certain words in the Salish language have not always met with success. Sealth, the leader of the Duwamish and a few other Puget Sound tribes, became known as Chief Seattle; *gwi-duc*, the Nisqually word for "dig deep," was transformed into geoduck, the giant edible clam; and Saskahevas was transformed into Sasquatch. Equally bothersome, the authenticity of several transcripts has been questioned—it's too easy, even for trained ethnographers, to misguidedly alter the story line or put words in the narrator's mouth. One egregious example of the latter relates to Chief Seattle's famous speech about the environment, that "Every part of this earth is sacred to my people." It is believed to have actually been written around 1970 by a man named Ted Perry, hired by the Southern Baptists to produce a film about pollution.

Aside from getting it right, anthropologists and others must wrestle with their own culture's rigid distinction between fable and fact. The tribes may not necessarily share this distinction, or not in the exact same way. As such, we tend to put information gleaned from Native stories into one of two boxes—real/natural or mythical/supernatural. The end result is that scientists don't know how to categorize Native American testimony about the Sasquatch—and all too often, they jettison it.

"These stories do not constitute proof that the Bigfoot [Sasquatch] exists," explains Kathy Moskowitz Strain. "They simply represent a collection of stories told by Native people about a humanlike giant, who at times is a man-eating cannibal, horrible monster, thief, a trickster, a helper, and in a few stories, our creator."

Amen to that.

ADVENTURES IN CRYPTOZOOLOGY

Turning our attention away from the time-honored wisdom of tribal elders, let's return to the comparatively recent conceits of modern science. It's time to introduce another new word: *cryptozoology*, the study of "hidden animals." This particular word was coined in the late 1950s by Bernard Heuvelmans, a French-Belgian zoologist. Heuvelmans wrote a thick book on the subject and cofounded the International Society of Cryptozoology, or ISC, in 1982.

The subjects of a cryptozoologist's quest, to use the ISC's definition, are "animals of unexplained form or size, or unexpected occurrence in time or space." Collectively known as cryptids, these animals include "Nessie" the Loch Ness monster, and Moklele-mbembe, a miniature long-necked dinosaur, reportedly from the central African swamps. There's also the ferocious chupacabra, or goat sucker, of the Caribbean and, of course, the Abominable Snowman, or yeti, of the Himalaya range. Known for its large footprints and loud vocalizations, the Sasquatch of the Pacific Northwest is likely the cryptid that readers of this book are most eager to meet someday.

By nature, most cryptozoologists are freethinkers. But far from being an assortment of bug-eyed weirdos, many are respected scientists, tenured university professors, or both. Some are self-taught experts— mountain climbers, trekkers, big game hunters, and others with extensive firsthand knowledge of a region's unique and oftentimes secretive fauna. Collectively, they have divvied up their world of hidden animals into six subcategories:

- **Unconfirmed**: An animal's existence is alleged but has not demonstrated.
- **Disputed**: The body of evidence does not support the fact of the animal's existence.

- **Proposed**: Evidence has been put forth but has not yet been accepted by the scientific community.
- **Confirmed**: Animals formerly classified as cryptids but whose existence has since been established.
- **Extinct**: Animals once thought to be extinct but that may, in fact, still exist as relict populations.
- **Hoax**: Deliberately crafted fakes that may have fooled somebody before the truth was revealed.

SOME SAY PSEUDOSCIENCE

Wikipedia describes cryptozoology as a pseudoscience, that is, a load of hogwash with a light dusting of science to make it palatable. Cryptozoologists think otherwise. They point out that, in many instances, the cryptid of yesteryear has become the commonplace critter at today's aquariums and zoos.

The okapi (*Okapia johnstoni*) is one of those cryptids whose "unconfirmed" status has been changed to "confirmed." A brown-and-white relative of the giraffe, this even-toed ungulate has been a familiar figure to the people living in its homeland, the Ituru rain forest of Kenya. However, in the nineteenth century it was still unknown to Western scientists. The okapi was established scientifically in 1901, after a British adventurer shipped an okapi carcass to London, putting an end to several decades of debate over this mammal's existence.

Similarly, the eastern gorilla (*Gorilla beringei*), the largest living primate on earth, wasn't formally described and given a scientific name until 1914. Surely, the human inhabitants of Uganda and Rwanda knew these human-sized apes were around: an adult male eastern gorilla can be five and a half feet tall and weigh 450 pounds. Females are smaller, but even they are not likely to be overlooked.

What about those adorable black-and-white pandas at the zoo? The giant panda (*Ailuropoda melanoleuca*) was unknown outside of China until 1869, when a French missionary and naturalist, Père Armand David, wrote about one he had seen that had been killed by hunters. Nearly fifty years passed before a second Westerner, this time a German zoologist, saw a living specimen of the panda—in this case, a panda cub he purchased while traveling through China and Tibet.

Cryptozoological discoveries in the ocean have been much more outrageous than on land. Number one on the list of the top ten cryptids is the megamouth shark (*Megachasma pelagios*), an eighteen-foot-long deepwater fish with a bioluminescent lining around its mouth—it glows in the dark. This seemingly hard-to-miss shark had somehow eluded science for centuries and was only discovered in 1976, when a specimen was accidentally snagged by the sea anchor of a US Navy ship stationed in the Hawaiian islands. Ichthyologists are currently uncertain where to place this one-of-a-kind shark on the fish family tree.

Second place goes to the coelacanth, a so-called living fossil. This primitive lobe-finned fish was presumed to have become extinct around eight million years ago. That is, until 1938, when a museum curator bought one from a South African fisherman. It was, without question, the catch of the day. Since then, several dozen coelacanths have been brought up from the depths.

"Men really need sea-monsters in their personal oceans," John Steinbeck wrote in his book *The Log from the Sea of Cortez*. In the same book, Steinbeck declared, "An ocean without its unnamed monsters would be like a completely dreamless sleep."

The casebooks for certain cryptids have remained open for years, decades, and in some instances, centuries. Take the onza, for example. Some cryptozoologists think this long, thin, large-eared mammal, reportedly seen in the Sierra Madre Occidental range of Mexico, is a subspecies of puma (*Puma yagouaroundi*). Or, it could be an entirely new species, join-ing the puma and the jaguar (*Panthera onca*) as that region's third big cat. To date, there have been numerous sightings of onzas and some physical remains—a partial skull and a few bones—but not enough on which to argue a case.

HEARD OF HOMINOLOGY?

Not content to be called a cryptologist, Russian researcher Dmitri Bayanov invented a new title for his particular field of study—hominology. That's the study of cryptids that are dimly or directly related to us.

It makes sense that a Russian would be fascinated by such things. There have been many purported sightings of humanlike beings (homi-nids) throughout Bayanov's nation. The Almas, for instance, is said to be a hairy, five-foot-tall wild man who has neither tools nor a discernible language, and is believed to inhabit caves in the Caucasus Mountains of southeastern Russia.

Supposedly, the Almas also inhabit the Pamir mountains—a range that crosses parts of Uzbekistan, Pakistan, Afghanistan, and China. It was here, in 1925, that Mikhail Stephanovitch Topilski, a major-general in the Soviet army, had a run-in with one these hominids. At that time, Topilski's team of soldiers was busy tracking down anti-Soviet rebels. While search-ing for rebel encampments in the craggy mountain slopes, they happened upon the fresh corpse of an Almas. To quote Topilski, as presented in the book *Still Living? Yeti, Sasquatch, and the Neanderthal Enigma* by anthro-pologist Myra Shackley: "At first glance, I thought the body was that of an ape. It was covered with hair all over. But I knew there were no apes in the Pamirs. Also the body itself looked very much like a man."

Of this strange man-beast's face, Topilski continued: "The eyes were dark and the teeth were large and even and shaped like human teeth. The forehead was slanting and the eyebrows were very powerful. The protruding jawbones made the face resemble the Mongol type of face. The nose was flat, with a deeply sunk bridge. The ears were hairless and looked a little more pointed than a human being's with a longer lobe. The lower jaw was very massive."

That description brings to mind another hominid, the so-called Neanderthal man (*Homo neanderthalensis*), believed to have gone extinct or, perhaps, to have been assimilated into our own gene pool thirty thousand to forty thousand years ago. To some cryptozoologists, Topilski's discovery fits the profile of *Homo erectus*, commonly known as Java or Peking Man. One of several such run-ins with unusual upright-walking entities in the Pamirs, the Almas incident is a classic illustration of how a relict population of hominids, formerly thought to be extinct, could be living in isolation, at a seemingly safe distance from the civilized world.

Yikes! The Yeti

Most people are familiar with the Abominable Snowman, or yeti, of the Himalaya. The yeti has been the focus of intense cryptozoological scrutiny since 1921. In that year, Lieutenant Colonel Charles K. Howard-Bury and his fellow expeditioners on Mount Everest found some unexplained footprints, three times the size of a man's, in the snow. Subsequent Everest expeditions brought back additional information about the yeti. Over time, a general impression of this hominid emerged. The yeti was said to live in caves at altitudes between fourteen thousand and twenty thousand feet or on lower altitudes in the impenetrable thickets of the montane wilderness.

Although there's disagreement about the yeti's physical form, the general consensus is of an upright-walking creature, four to six feet tall, with sloping shoulders, and a somewhat hunched-over stance. Observers say the yeti's face is similar to an ape's or a monkey's. Its body is covered in reddish, golden, or snowy white hair, depending on whose description you choose to accept.

The name Abominable Snowman is reduced to an acronym, ABSM, in Ivan T. Sanderson's historic work *Abominable Snowmen: Legend Come to Life*. The book's subtitle pretty much says it all: *The Story of Sub-Humans on Five Continents from the Early Ice Age Until Today*. Incidentally, Sanderson

A YETI TALE

Since 1921, when Charles Howard-Bury led the first British expedition to Mount Everest, the Sherpa people of northeastern Nepal and Tibet have been considered the best guides to their Himalayan mountain homeland. The name *Sherpa* has become synonymous with porter or expedition guide.

The Sherpas have also earned reputations as experts on the Abominable Snowman, or yeti as it is called in their language. Some of their stories are frightening; others are humorous or enlightening. All of them are insightful, helping us to become more familiar with this elusive second cousin of the Sasquatch.

The following story, adapted from *Lore and Legend of the Yeti* by Kesar Lall, establishes the close but not always coexistent nature of the relationship between Sherpa and yeti.

Several yeti families once lived in the mountains near the Sherpa village of Namche Bazaar in Nepal. During the day, they sat around, watching the villagers as they worked in their fields. But at night, after the villagers had returned to their homes, the yetis took to the fields, uprooting newly planted crops and trampling the older ones.

Afraid of the yetis, the villagers remained in their homes waiting for daybreak, when they could replant their >>>

<<< *fields. This went on for months, until one of the Sherpas hatched a plan. He recruited his neighbors to stage a mock celebration out in the fields.*

As the yetis watched from afar, the neighbors sang, danced, and drank pots of chang—a local beer made from millet. To the yetis, it looked like everyone was having a good time. Under the influence of the chang, the villagers laughed and joked with each other. Suddenly a fight broke out among the intoxicated villagers. Push turned to shove, and soon they were slashing and striking each other with toy swords made of wood.

The fight ended as quickly as it began. The villagers returned to their houses, leaving behind their chang pots and toy swords. Or so it seemed to the yetis. As night fell, the yetis were fast asleep, but some of the villagers stayed awake. They snuck back to the fields, where they refilled the chang pots with strong liquor and replaced the wooden weapons with real ones made of steel. Then, they crept back to their homes and waited for dawn and the yetis' return.

When the yetis came back, intent on making more mayhem, they discovered the chang pots and swords. They began to drink, just as they had seen the Sherpas do. Next, they grabbed the swords, waving them in the air, further imitating the villagers. However, this time, all that stabbing and slashing was for real.

By day's end, there was nary a yeti left standing. Thanks to their clever game of "monkey see, monkey do," the villagers could now tend their crops without being harassed by the yetis.

was also the author of *How to Know the North American Mammals*, published ten years before his book on Abominable Snowmen. Alas, this pocket-sized field guide to North American mammals contains no mention whatsoever of the Sasquatch.

Yeti stories continue to be told, but the stream of evidence in support of this apelike cryptid has all but dried up. In 2014, a collection of thirty hair samples from what researchers called "anomalous primates" (including the yeti) failed to pass some fairly rigorous laboratory testing. The genetic makeup of these samples was easily ascribed to a range of other critters, including black bears, sheep, mule deer, porcupines (and *you* thought they only had quills), and humans. Nonetheless, the test results revealed that two of the three purported yeti hair samples, one from Ladakh, India, the other from Bhutan, came from a "mystery bear" whose closest genetic affinity is to an ancient polar bear (*Ursus maritimus*) known to have lived forty thousand years ago. The samples may also have been from a previously unrecognized species of bear or, perhaps, from a polar bear–brown bear cross. Famed mountaineer Reinhold Messner, who was once mistaken for a Yeti himself, favors this latter theory. There's undoubtedly plenty of fuel for many late-night discussions among the world's cryptozoologists.

A Host of Hominids

Judging from the reports, there are many more hominids on our planet than there are hominologists to study them. The Agogwe of Tanzania is described as a pint-sized man with long arms and body covered in russet-colored hair. The long hair is said to conceal reddish-yellow skin. Bernard Heuvelmans proposed that this being was a "proto-Pygmy," possibly descended from the extinct hominid *Australopithecus*, a distant ancestor of ours whose scientific name means "southern ape."

In Southeast Asia and China, a species of bear-man, variously known as the Kung-Lu, the Dsu-The, the Ggin-Sung, and the Tok, has a reputation

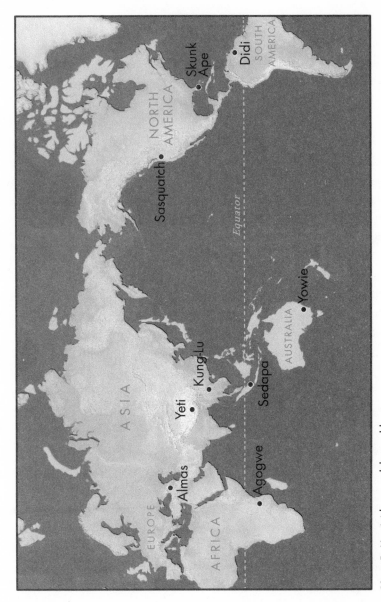

Map 1. Hominids around the world

as a bloodthirsty predator. Its prey includes any human, adult or child, it stumbles across. There's also the Orang Pendek or Sedapa of Sumatra, which has left its humanlike footprints in the dense forests of Sumatra, and the Yowie of Australia, one of several hominids in aboriginal lore.

Similar beings are also alleged to inhabit North, Central, and South America; although the newness of these lands in geological terms makes it less likely that a protohuman would be found in these places. Tales of the Didi, a five-foot-tall creature of the Guianas, have been circulating since the sixteenth century, when Sir Walter Raleigh wrote, "For my owne part I saw them not, but I am resolved that so many people did not all combine or forethinke to make the report." In other words, he didn't think that so many eyewitnesses could be making this stuff up.

Not far from Raleigh's colonial outpost in Virginia, in the wetlands and bogs of Florida, Louisiana, and eastern Texas, is a supposed hominid called the Skunk Ape. Pre–World War II reports of this hominid painted a picture of a chimpanzee-sized creature that smelled rather foul and that walked on all fours, leaving knuckle prints as well as footprints in the mud. However, since the late 1970s, the Skunk Ape's portrait has become supersized. It is now reported to be seven feet tall, weighing 300 pounds and giving off an aroma that has been compared to rotten eggs, skunk spray, and cow flatulence combined.

ENTER THE SASQUATCH

As we've seen, people have been talking about this book's subject, the Sasquatch, since the earliest days of human settlement. The written and oral testimonies of more recent arrivals to the Northwest have been valuable sources of information about the Sasquatch's appearance and behaviors. In several of these depositions, the Sasquatch is presented as malevolent. Some of these stories seem a trifle far-fetched. In one tale from the mid-1920s, a man claimed to have been carted off in his sleeping bag and dropped at the feet of a family of four Sasquatches. As their captive, he lived with this family of three adults and one juvenile for six days, sharing meals and sleeping in the out-of-doors until he could escape.

An even older report from the *Colonist* newspaper of Victoria, British Columbia, described how a railroad crew pursued and eventually captured what the paper described as "truly half man and half beast."

> *'Jacko' as his captors have described the creature is something of the gorilla type, standing about four feet seven inches in height and weighing 127 pounds. He has long black strong hair and resembles a human being with one exception, his entire body, excepting his hands or paws and feet is covered with glossy hair about one inch long. His forearm is much longer than a man's and he possesses extraordinary strength, as he will take a hold of a stick and break it by wrenching it or twisting it, which no man living could break in the same way.*

What became of Jacko is not known. Some speculate that he was shipped in a crate to a sideshow in England and perished en route. Others suggest he was acquired by showman P. T. Barnum and put on public display as Jo-Jo the Dog-Faced Boy. Still others maintain the entire thing was a fabrication—a fanciful solution to a slow news day.

Here's another golden oldie. One day in August 1958, Jerry Crew, a bulldozer operator for Wallace Construction, saw prints of huge naked feet that circled and walked away from his rig in a remote part of Humboldt County, California. The *Humboldt Times* in Eureka ran a front-page story and a photo showing one of the prints. The paper identified the track as that of "Bigfoot." As you'd expect, the story was quickly picked up and disseminated in newspapers across the country. Soon Bigfoot was a household word.

The problem was that those tracks were fakes. According to the children of the late Ray Wallace, their dad had sought out a friend, asking him to carve some sixteen-inch-long feet out of alderwood. Then he and his brother Wilbur strapped them on and set out to make some mischief, fooling Crew and the other members of the road crew with their footwork.

"This wasn't a well-planned plot or anything," Michael Wallace, one of Ray's sons, told Timothy Egan, writing for the *New York Times*. "It's weird because it was just a joke, and then it took on such a life of its own that even now, we can't stop it." But the younger Wallace was also encouraging to would-be Sasquatch seekers. "As long as Dad was alive, he was Bigfoot," he told Egan. "He may be gone, but I still think people should keep looking."

In his book *Bigfoot: The Yeti and Sasquatch in Myth and Reality*, primatologist John Napier divided Sasquatch footprints into two types. One type resembles large human feet; the other looks like what Napier termed an "hourglass" shape. This second type has a "waisted" appearance and toes that are more or less uniform—in short, the characteristics of Ray Wallace's alderwood strap-ons.

To Napier, the differences between them were significant, well beyond the range of the normal variation you'd expect to see in one species of animal. It's not unusual to find such variation in nonessential attributes such as hair color, eye color, or ear length. But when it comes to things like locomotion, there's not a lot of wiggle room in the way that feet, legs, and ankles work.

After much thought, Napier determined that the hourglass-shaped footprints were fakes. In the case of the Humboldt County tracks, he was right. However, it should be noted that many purported Sasquatch or Bigfoot prints have been found stamped into the soil of Humboldt County—and very few of them are matches to the historic ones made by Ray and Wilbur.

JOHN NAPIER'S BEST-KNOWN STUDENT

During his lifetime, John Napier distinguished himself as a primatologist, specializing in the study of primate hands and feet. He was the director of the Primate Biology Program at the Smithsonian Institution and a visiting professor of primate biology at the University of London. Published in 1973, his book, *Bigfoot: The Yeti and Sasquatch in Myth and Reality* remains a valued tome.

Napier's fame was eclipsed by that of his student, Jane Goodall, who attended Napier's classes on primate anatomy in the 1950s. Goodall went on to become the world's foremost authority on chimpanzees. Initiated in 1960, her Gombe chimp observation effort is considered the world's longest-running continuous wildlife research project. Through the Jane Goodall Institute, cofounded with philanthropist Genevieve di San Faustino in 1972, she has become equally well known as a conservationist and a staunch defender of human rights. The institute's Roots and Shoots program supports and encourages numerous citizen science projects for young people around the world.

Goodall has a fondness for all primates, including the Sasquatch and yeti. Speaking on National Public Radio's *Science Friday* in 2002, she told host Ira Flatow, "Maybe they don't exist, but I want them to." Ten years later, she repeated her views, telling a reporter from the *Huffington Post*, "I'm fascinated and would actually love them to exist."

Last of an Ancient Lineage?

Nobody knows how many species of humanlike primates have existed in the past. The fossil record tells us that many species of tailless, upright-walking beings had evolved after our human and ape ancestors went their separate ways. A favored theory among hominologists is that the Sasquatch's lineage may be traced to one of those ancestral stocks, possibly *Homo erectus*. Neanderthal man, *Homo sapiens neanderthalensis*, is also a prime candidate for the position of the Sasquatch's great-great-great-great-great grand pappy. So is *Australopithecus robustus*, whose name, translated from Latin, means the "robust ape from the southern land."

Genetic studies of fossilized Neanderthal skeletons indicate that this genus is more recent than the others, having died out, or become assimilated with our own genetic heritage through inbreeding, some thirty thousand to forty thousand years ago. That's practically the day before yesterday in evolutionary terms, and some researchers posit that relict populations of these or other hominid forebears have survived in remote regions of our planet, giving rise to the numerous tales of hairy, brutish beings told by humans in so many parts of the world.

When the conversation turns to relict populations of animals previously thought to have gone extinct, there's one candidate for Sasquatch-dom that stands, quite literally, head and shoulders above the rest. That creature is *Gigantopithecus*, quite possibly the largest primate ever to have walked the earth. From scientific reconstructions based on limited fossil evidence, this supersized ape stood nearly ten feet tall and weighed in excess of 1100 pounds.

"Now we're talking!" some of you might say—that's about the same height and weight as the Sasquatch, at least in the majority of eyewitness reports. Fossilized remains of this brute—a collection of extremely large teeth and a few mandibles from Vietnam and China—have been dated to a time six to nine million years ago, in the Pliocene epoch. However, it's possible that some populations may have survived into the late mid-Pleistocene epoch, roughly five hundred thousand years ago and perhaps as recently as one hundred thousand years before the Modern Age. On that

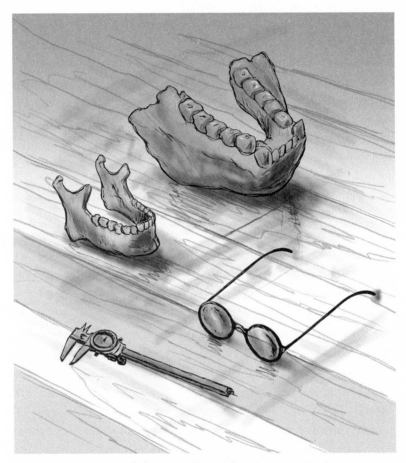

Figure 2. Comparisons of a human jawbone *(left)* and a reconstructed *Gigantopithecus* jawbone *(right)*

time line, *Gigantopithecus* and our immediate *Homo sapiens* ancestors could have shared the same turf. If such a thing as ancestral memory does exist, there may be some rather murky remembrances of this giant in our collective unconscious.

Several noted hominologists have theorized that *Gigantopithecus* may have vanished from its home range in Southeast Asia, perhaps having been hunted down or simply outcompeted by our own species. However, far from fading away, these beings merely expanded their range during the Pleistocene Ice Age, crossing the land bridge that briefly connected Alaska and Siberia to find fresh habitats in the New World. And that, they say, is what people are seeing today: a relict population of this King Kong–like entity, holed up in the wilds of the Northwest.

Of course, there are problems with such theorizing. For one thing, the patterns of wear on fossilized *Gigantopithecus* teeth indicate that, like the giant panda of China, *Gigantopithecus* may have subsisted solely on a diet of bamboo shoots, stems, and leaves. It's a bit of a leap to imagine this animal taking leave of the extensive bamboo stands of China and eking out an existence in the newly revealed (and bamboo-free) forests of the Pacific Northwest.

Furthermore, because no limb bones or pelvises of *Gigantopithecus* have been unearthed, the question of whether this brute walked erect remains open. With its closest living relative, the orangutan, being a knuckle-walker, the odds are better than fifty-fifty that *Gigantopithecus* was one, too. On the other side of the betting table, we have people like the late Grover Krantz, an anthropology professor at Washington State University, who argued that the wide U-shaped jawbone of *Gigantopithecus* was designed so this creature's skull could perch atop an erect spinal column.

In Krantz's view, Sasquatch and *Gigantopithecus* were one and the same. He proposed that the name *Gigantopithecus blacki*, one of three *Giganto* species known to science, be applied to the Sasquatch. The International Commission on Zoological Nomenclature turned down the proposal, but that didn't stop Krantz. A few years later, he came up with an alternative name, *Gigantopithecus canadensis*, which was also rejected by the ICZN.

A curious side note: after Krantz's death in 2002, the colorful and controversial anthropologist had his skeleton and that of Clyde, his beloved Irish wolfhound, mounted and put on display at the Smithsonian Institution's National Museum of Natural History.

FOLDEROL AND FAKES

So why is cryptozoology considered a pseudoscience? Most likely because from time to time, its practitioners disregard the agreed-upon procedures of the modern scientific method. The foundation of the scientific method involves formulating a hypothesis—that is, a proposed explanation for something—and, then, conducting experiments to test whether it is wrong or right.

The hypothesis must relate to the known world. In other words, it needs to be based on observable phenomena that occur in nature, not in some fictionalized place, like where the *Matrix* takes place. Step outside of that construct—for instance, by saying that a creature exists without offering real, tangible proof—and you've got a problem on your hands, scientifically speaking.

If anything has contributed to cryptozoology's reputation as a pseudoscience, it's the multitude of exaggerated claims, false or misidentified sightings, and outright hoaxes that have plagued this field of study. Naturally, it hasn't helped that several key pieces of cryptozoological evidence, put forth in earnest as fact, have not withstood the test of time—or of close scrutiny.

A large number of people, scientists among them, once thought that an iconic black-and-white photograph of a long, plesiosaurlike neck rising up out of the water was proof that Nessie, the fabled Loch Ness monster, was real. Imagine their shock when Christian Spurling admitted on his deathbed that the creature in the picture was a fake. Spurling and his stepfather had taken a toy submarine, fastened a carved wooden head and neck to it, and launched it from the shore into the loch. A photo was snapped and submitted to Britain's *Daily Mail* newspaper. You know the rest.

Hominology has been especially hard-hit by falsehoods, some perpetrated by otherwise highly regarded scientists. Few have been as widely discussed as the Piltdown Man forgery, the work of an unlikely team that included several British scientists, a Jesuit priest, and, legend has it, none other than Sir Arthur Conan Doyle, creator of the classic Sherlock Holmes series of books.

In the early 1900s, this odd coterie faked the discovery of what they claimed was the missing link between humans and apes. In truth, their find consisted of the jawbone of an orangutan attached to a cranium belonging to a medieval human. The purpose of such a fib? It's been said that the team of Brits wanted to prove to the world that the first *Homo sapiens*, our immediate ancestor, had evolved in *their* country, not one of those "lesser" nations in Africa or Asia. The skull's veracity was hotly debated among archeological and paleontological circles throughout the world, until 1953, when the truth about Piltdown Man was revealed by reporters from *Life* magazine—four decades after the bogus noggin had been fabricated.

In the 1960s, Frank Hansen toured the Midwest with his attraction, the Minnesota Iceman, claiming that this specimen was "a man left over from the Ice Age." He charged twenty-five cents for a peek at this marvel, put on display at state fairs and shopping malls, entombed in a block of ice within a refrigerated glass coffin.

Accompanied by Ivan Sanderson, author of *Abominable Snowmen: Legend Come to Life*, cryptozoologist Bernard Heuvelmans drove to Hansen's farm in Rollingstone, Minnesota, to observe and photograph this frozen oddity. Both scholars were convinced that what they saw was genuine—so much so that Heuvelmans wrote a scientific paper, in which he named the creature *Homo pongoides*. Sanderson appeared on *The Tonight Show Starring Johnny Carson* during Christmas week in 1968. He told TV

Figure 3. Relative height estimates *(left to right)*: *Gigantopithecus*, Sasquatch, grizzly bear, and human

viewers about the Iceman, occasionally referring to it as "Bozo"—Hansen's nickname for the prehistoric man-beast.

Somehow, in the months that followed the visit, the body that the two cryptozoologists saw and authenticated was replaced by an entirely different specimen—this one a model, allegedly made of rubber by an "Imagineer," a special-effects master in the employ of the Walt Disney Studios, working in his free time. As expected, Hansen initially refuted this allegation, though he eventually admitted that there had in fact been a bait and switch. He said that the real Iceman had been withdrawn from public viewing by its owner, an anonymous millionaire. Or so the story goes . . .

A second great faker, Rick Dyer, claimed to have shot and killed a Sasquatch in September 2012. According to Dyer, he lured his victim within shooting range with marinated pork ribs from Wal-Mart fastened to trees in a forested area near San Antonio, Texas. He nicknamed the carcass "Hank." Samples of Hank's DNA were supposedly sent to a university in Washington State for analysis. Dyer hinted that the lab results confirmed that Hank represented an entirely new species of hominid.

He also announced plans to take Hank on the road. The tour was short-lived, with Dyer failing to find suitable venues for showing off his trophy. Skeptics demanded to see the DNA test results but were dismissed. Dyer engaged in rancorous discourse with fellow Sasquatch hunters and members of the press. In April 2014, the man, who once boasted that he was "the best Bigfoot tracker in the world," confessed on his Facebook page that Hank was a fake. "From this moment own [sic], I will speak the truth!" Dyer proclaimed to his online followers.

MOVIE MAGIC AND PRANK APPEAL

Why would people like Hansen or Dyer want to pull off such large-scale hoaxes? "It's simple," Alec Gillis, cofounder of Amalgamated Dynamics, Inc., a visual-effects company in Chatsworth, California, explained to me in a recent interview.

"Anyone who makes monsters for movies knows the value of a good prank," he explains. "As a species, we love it. We love watching it, we love doing it, and we love being pranked. And let's face it, we're also fascinated by the possibilities—with whatever mysteries the world might have in store for us."

Gillis knows plenty about the world's mysteries and then some. He and his partner, Tom Woodruff Jr., helped create movie

<<< monsters for titles such as *Aliens, Predator, Mortal Kombat* and, a personal favorite, *Starship Troopers.*

"Because of the increase in communication technology, our world has shrunk and become more familiar," he says. "This leads to a loss of the mystery and sense of wonder that our imaginations thrive on. Pranksters provide fuel for that imagination and now YouTube provides a global forum where we can gather and collectively marvel at the footage—or complain about its obvious fakery."

According to Gillis, it wouldn't take much to manufacture a high-quality Sasquatch suit. In a home workshop or garage, an inspired novice could fabricate a decent suit for a few hundred dollars, he says. However, for a Hollywood feature film, the sky's the limit budget-wise. A similar suit might cost hundreds of thousands of dollars.

As an example of a high-end Sasquatch getup, Gillis points to the costume used in director William Dear's film *Harry and the Hendersons.* This convincingly real piece was designed by Rick Baker, the special-effects wizard who also designed the ape costumes for the film adaptation of Dian Fossey's *Gorillas in the Mist,* and featured individually punched hairs and remote-controlled servomotors implanted within its latex mask to mimic the movements of facial muscles whenever the Sasquatch growled or grinned.

While filming *Harry and the Hendersons,* the already statuesque actor Kevin Peter Hall was made to look even taller with makeup and prosthetics adding ten inches to his seven-foot-three frame. But Hall was "more than just a guy in a suit," he once told an interviewer. "When people want big and a performance along with that big, I'm the one they call."

THE ROAD AHEAD

The information in this book is from an array of sources. Some of it is anecdotal—the tabloid articles and tales told by I-Seen-Ums, for example. Other information is cultural in nature, with roots tracing back to the earliest inhabitants of the Northwest and branches that extend to the *Finding Bigfoot* TV series, films such as *Harry and the Hendersons*, and many other representations of the Sasquatch in modern times. Together these sources provide context on what is broadly known about this being.

While the cultural legacy provides an important framework for our search for the Sasquatch, science provides the tools. As we learned, following the scientific method offers a path for furthering current research on this enigmatic creature. For instance, we covered why a type specimen of the Sasquatch is needed and what citizen science can do. With this background, and with the protocols covered in Part II, we can build on the research that has already been published in books, peer-reviewed journals, and other reputable sources. Science is itself a product of culture, and for our purposes, it is an especially important one, because knowing how to play by the rules of science is key to grassroots efforts in finding and studying the Sasquatch.

The day when the Sasquatch is formally recognized by science—when thought is given to its protection and well being, and when humanity is forced to reevaluate its place in the Primate family tree—may not be far off. Your findings and any subsequent investigations they inspire could very well tip the scales, ultimately leading to the widespread recognition that the entity known as the Sasquatch does in fact exist.

PART II

PROTOCOLS

"Do try to be sensible; it is not a particular sign of superiority to talk like a fool." —Maud C. Cooke, *Social Etiquette or Manners and Customs of Polite Society*

AFTER STUDYING THE FIRST PART of this book, you should know as much as anyone about the legend, lore, past alleged run-ins, and presumed next of kin of the Sasquatch. The next step is to prepare yourself—and your expedition team—for a trip into the wilderness. Now it's *your* turn to contribute to our understanding of this elusive being.

I encourage you to head outdoors in search of the Sasquatch, or at least in search of scientific evidence of its existence. Once you have gathered your notes and materials, in keeping with the methods of citizen science, you'll want to share your observations about the Sasquatch—where it lives, what it eats, and how it births and raises its young. That information could easily be fleshed out formally as a paper in a scientific journal or an article on a popular science website or in a magazine or posted online informally as a blog entry or a note on the Sasquatch Seeker's Field Manual website (http://davidgeorgegordon.com/sasquatch/). Along the way, you may find yourself formulating a hypothesis to describe one of the great mysteries of the Sasquatch: how it has successfully avoided detection by humans for so many, many years.

Your observations could result in our formally recognizing the Sasquatch as a legitimate biological entity. They could also reveal that there is no such thing as the Sasquatch, that what we've been seeing is really a bear. Either way, your contributions will be priceless, especially if they have been obtained with care, using standard scientific procedures. Only then will they be worth sharing with other citizen scientists and, when sorted, evaluated, and summarized, with the scientific community at large.

That's what this second part is about: ways to gather fresh evidence—indisputable proof that the Sasquatch does or does not exist.

MOUNTING A SEARCH

An effective Sasquatch-seeking effort will require the three Ps—planning, persistence, and patience. Even when it focuses on these, it's entirely possible that an individual or team in search of the Big Guy will come up empty-handed. If this happens, don't be discouraged. It's not like we're going on a fishing trip. As far as we know, the subject of our search is endowed with finely tuned senses and a fairly high intellect. It's not at all unusual for large-sized animals like this to evade their would-be observers. In Southeast Asia, biologists trailing the Sumatran rhinoceros (*Dicerorhinus sumatrensis*) have spent years in the very jungles where this shy and retiring rhino lives, without actually catching a glimpse of one.

Closer to home, the equally elusive grizzly bear (*Ursus arctos horribilis*) has extended its southern range, moving down from British Columbia and crossing the border into Washington State. To find out how many grizzlies had already made this move, state wildlife officials sent some of their best biologists into the mountains in search of bears. You would assume that a grizzly bear, like the Sumatran rhino, would be pretty easy to find. After all, we're talking about a mammal that can weigh about 800 pounds and stand nearly ten feet tall. Well, think again. The biologists found all sorts of secondary signs: claw marks on trees, footprints in mud, bits of fur, feces, and so on. But in five years of fieldwork, they never laid eyes on a single grizzly.

So enough with the buzz-killing talk. Suffice it to say that searching for the Sasquatch can be difficult and, at times, unrewarding work. However, if you can use the search as an excuse to visit the Pacific Northwest's state and provincial parks and national forest lands, the experience, whether fruitful or not, will still be fulfilling. Every time I immerse myself in nature, when I let myself relax and take in the myriad signals—the sights, sounds, and scents of the forest ecosystem—I am soon refreshed. It is my wish that as a well-trained Sasquatch seeker, you will have ample opportunities to enjoy this kind of peace.

It's possible to perform all the info-gathering tasks described in this book by yourself. However, it's advisable to include at least one other person to join you on your outings. Don't get me wrong—it's not because of the danger posed by an enraged adult male Sasquatch defending its territory or its young (see Sasquatch Aggression sidebar, below). Rather, a partner can bring an extra set of eyes and ears into play, finding signs of the Sasquatch that you may overlook by yourself. As important, a companion can also provide backup support, helping you return to the base camp in the event of an ankle sprain or taking emergency measures if the injury is more severe. If that's not enough reason, one or more people who are on the trip with you can serve as corroborating witnesses, testifying on your behalf that a brush with a Sasquatch *did* occur, just like you said it did.

It is always wise to choose fellow expedition members with care. Avoid overly talkative, excitable types who are prone to exaggeration or, worse yet, are adept at bending the truth. Look for individuals with positive attitudes, firm ethics, clear senses of purpose, and plenty of common sense.

A two-person team may be fine for a day trip, but for longer excursions, it'll be necessary to include a bigger crew. On these extended outings, individuals may be assigned specific roles—medic, cook, records

SASQUATCH AGGRESSION

There is actually no authenticated evidence of an unprovoked attack by a Sasquatch on a human being. For the most part, stories of battles between man and man-beast are crusty and unconfirmed. One such classic is attributed to none other than President Theodore Roosevelt. Written in 1893, his book *The Wilderness Hunter* includes the purportedly true tale of an attack on two hunter-trappers by a hairy Sasquatch-like monster. One of the men was killed in the struggle, according to Roosevelt. The other fled the scene, rifle in hand.

Even harder to believe is the narrative of José Mariano Moziño, a naturalist traveling with explorer Juan Francisco de la Bodega y Quadra in 1792. Sharing his observations about life in what is now known as British Columbia, he wrote of "inhabitants of the mountainous country, of whom all have an unspeakable terror." Spookier than Freddy Krueger, "His howls fell to the ground those who hear them, and he smashes into a thousand pieces the unfortunate on whom a blow of his hands falls," Moziño maintained. Hyperbole? Perhaps.

That said, it's still a wise move to be careful around Sasquatches. Anything that big and strong, especially when put into a fight-or-flight situation, warrants extra caution. If you happen to cross paths with one, treat it with the same wary respect that you would accord >>>

keeper, scout, and so forth—to ensure that all expedition functions are performed with expertise.

SCIENTIFIC ADVICE

Another person to consider adding to your team is a person who can serve as the team's scientific advisor. At minimum, this person should be knowledgeable about the principles of general biology. She or he should also understand the basic "rules of the road" for gathering credible evidence,

<<< a black bear (*Ursus americanus*), wild boar (*Sus scrofa*), mountain goat (*Oreamnos americanus*), or any other potentially dangerous wild animal.

Keep a safe distance to avoid encroaching on its territory, and refrain from making any hand gestures or facial expressions that could be construed as threatening or defensive. For example, raising your arms above the head, inadvertently making yourself bigger than your new acquaintance, can be perceived by primates as a threat. Likewise, looking directly into another primate's eyes may come across as a challenge. Maybe this is why the Sasquatch is said to have hypnotic powers in several Native American tales—it's an indirect way of saying, "Don't stare at a Sasquatch." Similarly, a broad smile may be misconstrued as a grimace, suggesting to the Sasquatch that you are very afraid of it. Under no circumstances should you reach for a stick or anything else that might be confused for a weapon. And remember, it is unethical, and unlawful in at least one Northwest county, to shoot one. Since it is unlikely that you would be able to outrun a Sasquatch or best one in hand-to-hand combat, the safest tactic may be to hold your ground and wait for your new acquaintance to move on.

evaluating it, and presenting conclusions, for discussion and, ideally, acceptance, to others whose opinions count.

Recruiting such a person may be more difficult than it might seem. In general, established scientists and academicians may be wary of allying themselves with people who their peers have deemed unprofessional or eccentric. And believe me, within existing Sasquatch-seeking circles there are plenty of people who are unprofessional or eccentric, or both. Scientists may be fearful of jeopardizing their hard-earned reputations, while academics might fret about being denied tenured teaching positions because of their unorthodox beliefs. In either instance, gaining their trust may be an uphill battle at best.

It's also important to recognize that most scientists and scholars are extremely busy. Like babysitters, the best ones are often unavailable—if they're sitting around waiting for the phone to ring, how good can they really be? Plus their schedules may revolve around unyielding grant-funded research deadlines. Such commitments are often etched in stone years in advance, so getting one of these time-crunched individuals to respond to your emails or telephone messages can be nigh on impossible.

Thankfully, this is not always the case. While conducting research for this book, I spoke with several professors at major academic institutions who rose to the occasion and freely shared their expertise with me. Once you've gotten a foot in the door, so to speak, you may succeed in convincing such a person to help with your citizen science project. After you have gained their trust, this helpful soul may agree initially to serve as an informal advisor, reviewing your expedition's data-gathering plan. Later, once you have demonstrated your team's ability to collect new information that can withstand scientific review, your advisor may offer to help write, edit, and submit your findings to a scientific journal. He or she might eventually share laboratory equipment or even agree to participate as a team member on an upcoming trip.

ESSENTIAL EQUIPMENT

In any Sasquatch search, your safety and that of your team members must always be a prime concern. Whether embarking on a day hike or a week-long wilderness trek, don't leave home without the Ten Essentials, the minimum for guaranteeing the well-being of each person, in the event that things don't go as planned.

The Ten Essentials according to the systems approach developed by The Mountaineers are:

1. Navigation (map and compass)
2. Sun protection (sunglasses and sunscreen)
3. Insulation (extra clothing)
4. Illumination (headlamp or flashlight)
5. First-aid supplies (including a whistle or signal mirror)
6. Fire (firestarter and matches or a lighter)
7. Repair kit and tools (including knife)
8. Nutrition (extra food)
9. Hydration (extra water)
10. Emergency shelter (tarp, tent, or bivy sack)

Other items may not qualify as essential; nonetheless, they will vastly improve the chances of achieving a Sasquatch expedition's express goal.

1. Field journal notes and data-gathering forms
2. Still or video camera
3. Audio recorder
4. Handheld GPS device
5. Binoculars and magnifying glass
6. Fifty-foot and ten-foot tape measures or yardstick
7. Plastic, resealable food-storage bags (several sizes)

8. Rubber gloves and lightweight disposable cotton gloves
9. Letter-sized envelopes
10. Tweezers
11. Casting medium, mixing cups, and tools; or cans of aerosol foam and cardboard
12. Nonreactive plastic jars
13. Ethanol
14. Plastic trash bags
15. Harmonica

That may seem like a lot of stuff, but by bringing along a full-featured smartphone, the first four items can be removed from the list. Still, if you intend to make higher quality audio recordings or take digital photos or videos of subjects at a distance of more than six feet, the capabilities of a smartphone may be insufficient. Battery life can also be an issue. If you're outside of cell phone range, set your smartphone to "satellite" mode. For outings longer than twenty-four hours, one or more storage batteries may also be needed for backup power.

The items on this second list can easily fit in a medium-sized backpack or, with some spatial planning skills, a couple of day packs (yet another good reason to travel with a companion—two day packs). Most of them will be familiar to you, but a few require explanation. The value of trash bags, for instance, is vastly underrated: They can help you have a no-impact wilderness experience. Just as important, they allow you to clean up after less considerate adventurers, stashing their litter until it can be properly disposed of elsewhere. Guidance on casting materials and the related accessories for making an impression of a footprint cast can be found later in this chapter, in Making a Footprint Cast. Suggestions for capturing Sasquatch vocalizations and other sounds are in Capturing Sounds. The rubber gloves are for picking up Sasquatch scat (see Collecting Scat).

The harmonica? You'll have to read the following section, Tips to Improve Your Odds, to learn more.

Of course, for extended trips, you'll also need to bring the usual supplies—a tent, sleeping bag, air mattress or pad, cookware, tarp, and any home comforts, including this book. An abundance of advice about enjoying the outdoors can be found in print and online, so let's move on and discuss the data-gathering activities you'll engage in during your expedition.

TIPS TO IMPROVE YOUR ODDS

Finding a Sasquatch or its signs appears to be largely a matter of luck, even for people who've made a life's work of it. For instance, the team from *Finding Bigfoot* has had a few near misses but little else, even after several successive seasons in hot pursuit. On the other hand, there are many examples of people like Matthew Johnson, a licensed psychologist from Grants Pass, Oregon, who, without intending to, nearly urinated on a Sasquatch while hiking with his family one summer afternoon (see Oregon Caves National Monument, Oregon, in Part III). Indeed, the majority of eyewitness accounts begin with someone walking in the forest or driving their car on a lonely stretch of road, minding their own business, when they were lucky enough to be given a good look at the wild man of the woods in all his primal glory. With this in mind, I confess that it's beyond the scope of this field manual to offer exact and in-depth instructions for locating a Sasquatch in its natural habitat.

That said, there are several ways to improve your chances while Sasquatch seeking. The first is to look online for areas with a history of human and hominid interactions. Several websites maintain comprehensive databases with recent sightings or so-called footprint incidents, and these can offer hints about where to begin looking for additional clues. Likewise, a simple web search for "recent Bigfoot sightings" can yield several prime suggestions for places worthy of further investigation on foot.

See the Resources in the back of this book for a list of the most prominent Sasquatch websites.

Identifying the trends in prior sighting reports can also point you to prime Sasquatch-seeking locales. A high number of sightings have taken place near hot springs, in cleared areas around power transmission lines, and in proximity of large caves. The logic is that these places provide sources of food, shelter, and heat for these large and presumably warm-blooded beings.

"Powerlines represent one of the few places that sunlight reaches the forest floor and, therefore, gives rise to highly nutritious plants that deer and other herbivores need to survive," says Cliff Barackman of the *Finding Bigfoot* team. I'm prone to believe him. Barackman and his peers also posit that Sasquatches, like many other primates, live in small family groups and are territorial, actively defending home ranges that may extend over hundreds of miles. If true, this could make choosing a good starting point for mounting your Sasquatch expedition somewhat easier, especially where a succession of prior sightings can help to delineate the boundaries of a family's home turf.

One strategy for locating Sasquatches involves keeping on the move to cover as much ground as possible. Loop trails are extremely well suited for this kind of a search, as are backcountry bicycle and equestrian trails. A second approach is to establish a base camp from which a series of gradually larger sweeps of the vicinity can be made. Of this tactic, Robert W. Morgan's *Bigfoot Observer's Field Manual* maintains:

> *I like to make ever-widening concentric circles around my campsites to discover the most logical direction they might choose for a visit. I am usually wrong, but it keeps me thinking. Behave normally. Do not try to sneak up on the Forest Giants. Walk casually enough to allow your own observations but don't bother trying to sneak*

around because your actions may remind them of hunters and put them on guard. If your routine seems predictable and safe, they may eventually follow you back to your camp.

While you're at camp, Morgan suggests practicing yoga, pressing flowers, playing a guitar, and—yes—serenading yourself with a harmonica to create what he calls "a provocative routine" that will lure a naturally curious Sasquatch within range. Taking photos of wildflowers or scenery is a bad idea, he claims, as the shiny black housing and lens of a camera may resemble a hunter's rifle and scare away any nonhuman visitors.

Morgan also recommends that Sasquatch seekers maintain a degree of secrecy about the purpose of their day hikes or campouts. Rather than arousing curiosity and attracting onlookers who can get in the way of your quest, he advises that individuals explain to gas station attendants, shopkeepers, park rangers, and others that they are amateur wildlife photographers looking for some unusual shots. "You are not lying," he says, "so you can look them straight in the eye. And if they ask exactly what wildlife, tell them anything that you come across."

GATHERING EVIDENCE

People who think that Sasquatch seeking will be all thrills and fun may be surprised by the next few topics I cover. Admittedly, the excitement of the hunt can be great, whereas taking the time to thoroughly document your recent observations is considerably less dramatic. Nonetheless, it's your attempts to capture the details of this adventure—where you went, who you went with, what you heard, smelled, found, and saw—that will serve as the measure of your success or failure in the long run. Your records will be your legacy. If you want to enjoy the outdoors, hone your observation skills, and practice the techniques of field biologists, forensics specialists, and cryptozoologists, the following sections will help guide you on your way.

Figure 4. Field journal entries should be accurate, informative, and succinct.

WRITING FIELD NOTES

Field notes are a time-honored practice in the biological sciences, pre-dating the camera and other mechanical devices for establishing the scene. Accompanied by drawings, preserved specimens, pressed plants, and other forms of supporting evidence, field notes have been sufficient to establish the existence of thousands of plants and animals over the past four centuries. Compiled into journals and reproduced in print, the field notes of naturalists such as David Thompson, Alfred Russel Wallace, John James Audubon, Edward O. Wilson, and Charles Darwin have been instrumental in opening our eyes to previously unknown species throughout the world.

In this light, your field notes about the Sasquatch and its environs could be the single most important outcome of your expedition. As written chronicles, they will inform others about your attempts to find the Sasquatch, and tell them things about this being that they may never have heard before. As a guidebook, your collection of reports can assist others who may follow your lead, retracing your footsteps (and those of the Sasquatch) to reach the places where further information can be acquired. At its very least, your field notes can bring joy to cryptozoologists and other readers, enabling them to live through your expedition's highlights and low spots, vicariously, in the manner of the adventure travel genre—all thanks to your diligent efforts to put pen to paper.

Field notes should be written on the spot, usually but not always by hand, in indelible ink on durable (waterproof) paper. Many Sasquatch seekers favor a fine-point Sharpie for this purpose. It's a good idea to carry several of these with you, in case one becomes fouled or runs out of ink. For all entries, be as specific as possible. There's no such thing as being overly detailed. A person's memory is far from infallible—what's not committed to paper is likely to fade away and vanish over time.

At minimum, field entries should

- specify the day, date, and time;
- describe weather conditions;
- identify the point of origin, route, and destination;
- characterize the terrain;
- list all companions; and
- include any relevant notes.

TIPS FOR TAKING FIELD NOTES

As scientists say, "Seeing is not observing." The former comes naturally, but the latter takes discipline and training. Hone your abilities to make observations and to preserve them for later retrieval and study. The following tips will help you become a better field-note taker.

On an outing, carry extra notebooks and writing implements. If your original notebook is damaged or lost, be prepared to rewrite from memory, using a replacement notebook. Although not ideal, this stand-in is better than nothing at all.

Field notes should be usable and understandable by others. Strive to write legibly, even under duress. If writing in shorthand or using nonstandard abbreviations or symbols, be sure to include an explanatory key so that others (and for that matter, you) can easily decipher what you wrote.

Practice taking notes at home before making observations in the field. This will help you develop your own style of transcribing what you are seeing with speed and accuracy. Think about how you will organize your observation—for instance, chronologi-

>>>

When you get back from your trip, recopy any field notes into a note-book, diary, or journal set aside for this express purpose. Rewriting your notes this way will allow others to peruse chronologically what you have recorded. Under no circumstances should you discard the original field notes. You may need these to verify any details that are disputed at a later date.

MAINTAINING A CHAIN OF CUSTODY

All evidence—hair and scat samples, footprint casts, skeletal remains, and so on—must be collected and stored following standard procedures to ensure its integrity is not compromised. The protocols for maintaining a chain of custody will help establish that the evidence presented for study has not been accidentally or intentionally tampered with. The greater the chances that evidence has been altered by tampering, the less likely it is to

<<< cally or by topic. Notes that are disorganized will make it more difficult to interpret your findings.

Cultivate the habit of "interrogating the environment." As you survey your surroundings, ask yourself direct questions: What plants or animals am I seeing? What changes can I detect? What could explain those changes? What is my role in this?

Detailed drawings of sites and observable activities are invaluable aids. Practice before an outing by making a series of sketches of your home's living room, bedroom, or kitchen. Try sketching your friends or family members as they conduct their daily chores. See how quickly you capture the essential information on paper.

When reviewing your field notes, use color-coded pencils or markers to highlight the most important details. This tactic will help focus your attention, separating the most important information from any extraneous details.

be accepted by the scientific community. Thus, any evidence must be stored and handled with care.

Mold and mildew are especially harmful to organic materials. So are the oils, bacteria, and fragments of flaked skin that are usually present on human hands; these can seriously contaminate any samples for DNA testing, leading to the production of false results. For this reason, it's wise to wear lightweight disposable cotton gloves when handling samples in the field or at home.

As important, do not allow the evidence out of your possession until you can hand it over to an equally responsible person. To prove that you have monitored it properly, adequate records must be kept to establish this transfer of ownership. Documentation of such transfers—as a sample moves from the person who acquired it to subsequent examiners, to laboratory technicians, and so on—is called *chain of custody*. Plainly stated, all evidence must be in the possession of an identifiable person who can testify that he or she received it in a given condition at a given time from someone else or from the site where it was collected, and a paper trail that details these facts must be maintained. If this chain of custody cannot be arranged for beforehand, it is unwise to let the evidence out of your possession.

It's common for evidence to be tagged in a fashion that can demonstrate
- what the evidence is;
- when (date and time) and where the evidence was collected;
- who had contact with it; and
- what changes, if any, were made to the evidence, along with an explanation of why those changes were deemed necessary.

Note that we're not talking about the use of a fancy form here. A number five (4¾ inch x 2⅜ inch) manila shipping tag, obtainable at most office

Evidence: APPLE CORE WITH SUSPECTED SASQUATCH TOOTH MARKS
Date Collected: 8/18/14
Location: ORCHARD MCMENAMINS EDGEFIELD, TROUTDALE, OR
GPS coordinates: N47.6783· W-120.72815
By: JEFFREY COLE
Transfered to (name and date): DAVID GORDON 8/22/14
Notes: PRESERVATIVE (JACK DANIELS) REPLACED WITH ETHANOL

Figure 5. Sample evidence tag for establishing the chain of custody

supply stores, is ideal for this purpose. Affix the wire fastener on one of these tags to your material in a way that will not damage or alter the sample. Remember to update the information every time the sample changes hands. By following this procedure, you will have established a chain of custody and helped to pacify any scientists with nagging doubts about the authenticity of this particular piece of evidence.

TAKING PHOTOS AND VIDEOS

Good visual images of the Sasquatch are as rare as hen's teeth. Only a handful of still photographs and video recordings have been taken by seekers in the past, and many of these are brief, blurry, or both. Some of the best have been viewed repeatedly in hopes of gaining deeper insights into the nature of this being.

Unfortunately, films, videotapes, and digital files are all relatively easy to manipulate, making them appealing tools for the perpetrators of hoaxes. For this reason, experts must carefully examine them before they can be accepted as anything but fakes. Nearly fifty years after the now-familiar Patterson-Gimlin footage of Bigfoot at Bluff Creek, California (described in A Portrait of the Sasquatch, in Part I), was shared, experts are still in disagreement over its authenticity. There is uncertainty about the speed at which the film was taken, and several broken links in the chain of custody raise questions about how the raw footage was pro-cessed and passed from hand to hand (for more, see the Bluff Creek Blunders sidebar in Part III).

These deficits make it one of the most enigmatic (and some would say dubious) pieces of evidence that we have gathered to date. After round upon round of detailed analysis, the best that can be said of this footage is that no viewer has been able to find what many have called "the zipper in the suit." That's faint praise for what most people regard as the strongest visual proof of the Sasquatch's presence in the Northwest.

Hypothetically, the availability of digital cameras and lightweight video recorders should make it much easier to get the goods on the Sasquatch. After all, you'd think that the time-honored excuse—that the camera was out of film—would now be invalid. Still, one must have the presence of mind to start capturing images under duress. Plus, there's the issue of lim-ited battery life to further confound any documentarist's efforts. Sasquatch seekers are well advised to regularly recharge their equipment and, for long excursions, to carry extra batteries.

Katie Campbell is a multimedia journalist with EarthFix, a national public radio and television project covering environmental issues in the Northwest. Her subjects have included tribal canoeists, migrating salmon, the deadly Oso mudslide, and the removal of the Elwha Dam. These assignments have helped Campbell develop what she refers to as her sixth sense—the ability to lock in on the quintessential video moment a microsecond before it occurs.

The trick, says Campbell, is to be ready and steady. "Every minute counts, so you don't want to waste time fumbling through your gear," she says. "On the trail, your camera should never be in a day pack or backpack. Keep it in your hands or hanging from a strap around your neck."

Should you stumble across a Sasquatch, keep in mind this bit of practical advice from Campbell: "Take a few seconds to calm yourself," she says. "I usually take a few deep breaths. Then, when you're ready to hit 'record,' hold your breath and think of your body as a tripod—tuck in your elbows, holding your arms close to your body, and either kneel or lean against a tree."

To prepare for that big moment, Campbell also recommends that would-be videographers train themselves to shoot in distracting situations, such as sporting events or outdoor festivals. They should also take the time to learn their particular recorder's capabilities. In terms of reliability and affordability (from about three hundred to six hundred dollars), Campbell favors any of the Sony Handycam recorders or any of their other lightweight models that offer image stabilization, which enables the user to zoom while keeping the subject in focus.

Professional trackers theorize that the Sasquatch is especially adroit at staying out of sight—avoiding established hiking trails and game paths through the brush. They can see you well before you are aware of them, the trackers suggest. Therefore, some recommend using what are known as trail cameras—electronic devices that can be preset to operate remotely, gathering visual images when no human is around. Hunters commonly use these handy pieces of gear, often as part of a network of trail cameras, to gather information about the abundance of deer or other targeted prey.

Some of these cameras come with remotely operated flashes or infra-red systems for night photography. Others can transmit digital images directly to a computer, facilitating real-time monitoring of Sasquatch habitats.

Do they work? The internet is full of photos of supposed Sasquatches, taken surreptitiously by strategically placed trail cams. Alas, many of these are misidentifications of other animals such as bears or wild dogs. Like the Patterson-Gimlin footage, they must be viewed with healthy skepticism and an eye for the finest details.

CAPTURING SOUNDS

Whoops, howls, screams, and streams of gibberish—these sounds and more have been attributed to the Sasquatch. Many have been recorded and uploaded as MP3 files on the internet, along with commentaries describing the circumstances under which they were captured.

Among the most widely shared of these are audiotapes made by Ron Moorehead, a self-professed "adventurist, Bigfoot/Sasquatch researcher and entrepreneur." Moorehead released two CDs of supposed Sasquatch sounds that he and his companions first heard in the 1970s while at an outpost in a remote part of the Sierra Nevada of California. He believes that Sasquatches communicate using a fairly advanced form of language, poorly understood by humans. Other Sasquatch seekers maintain that their quarry communicates without vocalizations, loudly thumping on tree trunks to attract the attention of others of their own kind instead.

The problem is there's no way of verifying the authenticity of any of these recordings or oral reports. "I've spent a bit of time reviewing some of the acoustic 'evidence' a few groups have offered as proof of Bigfoot and found nothing of consequence other than bad attempts at falsification,"

Bernie Krause, a leading authority on animal sound recordings, informed me by email. Through his San Francisco firm Wild Sanctuary, Krause travels the world to record, archive, study, and share the sounds of the natural world. "Unless something considerably more substantial can be found, you'll need to count me in the highly skeptical camp," he confesses.

A second bioacoustics expert, Gordon Hempton of Indianola, Washington, told me by telephone that he also rules out most of the existing recordings he's reviewed. However, he suspects that the majority are not intentional fakes, merely misidentifications of other animals' sounds. To avoid any further gaffs, he advises would-be Sasquatch sound engineers to become well acquainted with the Cornell Lab of Ornithology's Macaulay Library online. At this site, you can gain access to the world's largest collection of wildlife audio (and video) recordings—the digitized sounds of more than one hundred seventy-five thousand species of invertebrates, reptiles, amphibians, birds, and mammals. Want to hear the cry of the striped skunk (*Mephitis mephitis*) or the American black bear? As a Sasquatch seeker, you may find these cries quite fascinating. Both are remarkably similar in tonal quality to some of the most convincing Sasquatch recordings—and both are available through the Macaulay Library's website.

Validating an audio recording is nearly impossible, according to Hempton. "Putting a time stamp on a recording doesn't mean much, because even that can be altered in postproduction," he says. "For that matter, with all of our sophisticated technologies, it's remarkably simple to fabricate all manner of convincing sounds."

However, a natural-sound specialist like Hempton or Krause can tell where and when a particular piece was recorded simply by listening to what's happening in the background. "Let's say you have a photograph with the Eiffel Tower in the background, you'd know at a glance it was taken in Paris," Hempton explains. "Likewise, if you're listening to a recording and there's the sound of a certain insect or frog in the background, you can tell right away if it's day or night, near a creek or pond and so on."

Although the professionals use highly sensitive microphones and expensive recorders, there's no real need to follow in their audio footsteps. For the layperson, Seattle-based sound engineer Charles Tomaras recommends the Zoom brand of portable recorders, which run from around a hundred dollars up to four hundred dollars. Protecting your microphone from wind is especially important when dealing with nature recording as is limiting noise from handling the gear—a side effect that comes from cranking up input volumes to capture sounds at great distances. A low-tech solution to the latter problem? Find a way to mount your gear to a stick that can be staked into the ground, avoiding any need to hold the recorder when in use, Tomaras says. And be sure to get "earwitness" reports in writing as additional proof that those grunts, groans, and knocking noises were genuine Sasquatch sounds.

INTERPRETING FOOTPRINTS

Bear tracks are commonly mistaken for Sasquatch footprints, and because the ranges of these animals presumably overlap, our first task is to learn to distinguish between the two to avoid misidentification issues.

A bear's front feet are short, with rounded pads that leave pear-shaped imprints in mud or soft ground. The rear feet are nearly twice as long as the front ones, with narrow heels and insteps that leave imprints that are very much like a human's in shape. When a bear walks, the left rear foot usually lands on the footprint made by the right front foot. To an inexperienced observer, this may give the impression of one very long print, and in his or her mind, that can only mean one thing—a Sasquatch walked here.

As long as you look closely, it's generally easy to rule out a bear's tracks, especially if you can isolate individual footprints as opposed to over-lapping ones. The rear footprint of a black bear, the most common bear

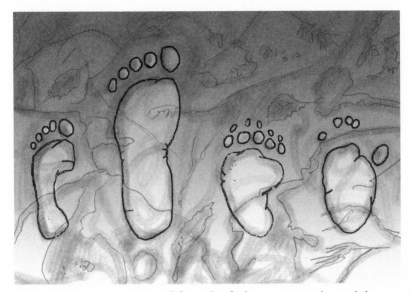

Figure 6. Footprint comparisons *(left to right)* of a human, Sasquatch, grizzly bear, and gorilla

species in the Northwest, seldom exceeds six inches. The vast majority of alleged Sasquatch tracks are longer than that. Even a rear footprint of a grizzly bear is less than fourteen inches—about the same as the smallest Sasquatch tracks reported.

Because a bear's claws are nonretractable, they can leave claw marks that are easily discerned in the majority of prints; claw marks in tracks is another way to rule them out as Sasquatch footprints. An exception would be when a bear has been treading on a very hard surface, in which case the claws will not make impressions. In that case, study the toe prints. A bear's five toes form a symmetrical arc—where the middle toe is the longest—unlike the footprints of a human or a Sasquatch. As mentioned earlier in this book, extremely large footprints with even-sized, equally spaced toes are probably fakes, left by pranksters or would-be perpetrators of hoaxes.

Now that we know what is *not* a Sasquatch print, here's what to look for in one that may be real. The Sasquatch is alleged to create prints that are flat, lacking the slightest sign of an instep or arch. The ball of the foot may be creased, suggesting unusual foot flexion. Another large crease may be seen in the region of the midfoot. This crease is known as a midtarsal break and is another product of flexion, thought to result from the foot being pressed firmly into the ground; as the heel is lifted, the forefoot pushes the soil or gravel toward the heel imprint, leaving a ridge.

Scientists can learn much about an animal from the footprint it leaves behind. Baron Georges Cuvier, the father of modern paleontology wrote about this in 1834. To illustrate his point, Cuvier used the example of a cloven-hoofed creature. Its footprint would suggest that the animal was a ruminant—a mammal that feeds on plant matter, which it obtains by lowering its head, clipping leaves and grasses with its front teeth (the incisors), and chewing thoroughly with its molars. "A single track therefore tells the observer about the kind of teeth, the kind of jaws, the haunches, the shoulder, and the pelvis of an animal which passed," Cuvier explained.

Similarly, students of primate anatomy can surmise much about the Sasquatch from a single footprint cast. They can infer even more from the study of a series of footprints, known as a *trackway* in biology. This trail can be interpreted to show how large the creature was, how quickly it was traveling, and whether it stopped along the way, perhaps to rest or survey its surroundings. Thus, whenever a team finds what it believes to be Sasquatch tracks, measurements should be taken of both the individual footprints and also the trackway found at a site.

The easiest way to do this is with a fifty-foot tape measure laid parallel to the trackway. A shorter tape measure can be placed near the heel of each print, perpendicular to the fifty-footer, to form a coordinate grid with an x-axis and a y-axis against which the angle of each track can be

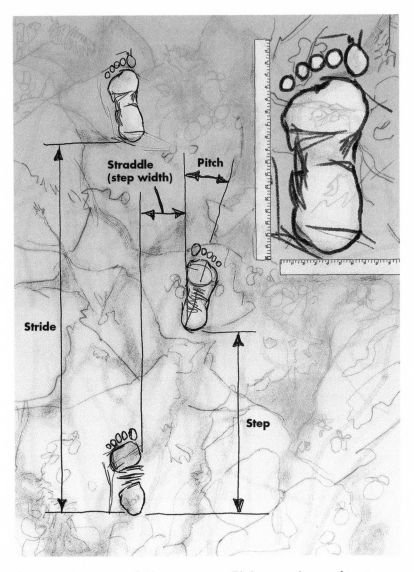

Figure 7. These common field measurements will help you analyze any footprints you find.

observed. For each footprint, take several photographs of this arrangement of tape measures. By photographing from different angles, using the naturally occurring patterns of light and shadows, the contours of each print can be more accurately assessed. You may need to use your camera's flash feature or a handheld flashlight to illuminate any footprints you've found. Later, you can make prints of the photos. By laying out the prints, using the inch marks on the longer tape measure as a guide, a photomosaic of the trackway can be assembled and studied.

Because the descriptive terms for the parameters of a trackway are often poorly understood, they are defined here:

- **Step:** The distance between the heel of one track and the heel of the next track.
- **Stride:** The distance between the same points on two consecutive tracks (in other words, the length of two steps).
- **Straddle or step width:** The distance between the same inside point on right and left heels.
- **Pitch:** The orientation of the axis of the foot to the line of travel.
- **Directionality:** The direction of travel.
- **Gait:** The speed of travel.
- **Toe kick:** The dirt plume left by the toes pushing off the ground as the track maker moves forward.

Making a Footprint Cast

Although photos can be adequate for documenting the sizes and contours of Sasquatch footprints, impressions made with casting materials can provide this information while also offering details such as depth and nuances in shape. For more visually oriented individuals, these casts may be easier to interpret—and their value as teaching tools to inspire other Sasquatch seekers is inarguable.

Numerous gypsum-based casting compounds, including Hydrocal, dental stone, and plaster of Paris, are suitable for taking track impressions. Several synthetic compounds are also available; however, they are often expensive—for example, Mold Star 16 FAST silicone, a favorite among forensics workers, costs approximately thirty dollars per unit and as many as five units may be needed to make a single impression of a large track.

Comparatively affordable (about twelve dollars for a twenty-five-pound sack) and relatively easy to acquire from hobby or craft supply stores, plaster is favored by many novice trackers. Its molecules of calcium sulfate hemihydrate bond easily with water, so it's also easy to mix and pour. However, plaster can crumble, so any casts made with this medium must be protected from rough handling or abrasion. For this reason, many experienced trackers prefer Ultracal 30, a very strong plaster formulation that sells for under twenty dollars per twenty-pound sack. Another advantage of Ultracal 30: unlike plaster, it doesn't expand or contract as it sets.

Materials:
- One-gallon plastic container with a screw-top lid
- A minimum of three pounds of Ultracal 30 or other casting medium
- Two quarts of water, unless there will be access to a nearby creek, stream, or other water source
- Three or more thirty-two-ounce plastic mixing cups
- Spatulas with durable handles
- Small wooden spoon
- Tweezers or knife for *carefully* removing pine needles or other debris from the track before casting
- Three-inch-wide plastic, metal, or cardboard strips from which to build dams to retain the plaster as it is poured

- Paper clips or binder clips to hold the edges of the strips together, forming a circle around each footprint
- Plastic trash bag for removing used cups, spatulas, plaster remnants, and any litter left from the casting process

Procedure (see figure 8):

1. With plastic, metal, or cardboard strips, create a circular dam around the footprint to retain the casting medium as it is poured to an appropriate depth. For large prints, use paper clips or binder clips to hold the edges of the strips together.

2. In one or more large (thirty-two-ounce) plastic cups, mix casting medium to the appropriate viscosity, following the manufacturer's instructions (generally one part water to three parts Ultracal 30 or two parts plaster). Strive for the consistency of a thin milk shake—a thicker mix will not always capture the desired degree of detail. Stir at an even pace to avoid folding bubbles into the mixture.

3. To pour the casting medium into a footprint, hold a spatula close to the footprint, and direct the stream onto the spatula's flat surface, thus lessening the possibility of eroding any fine detail in the delicate tracks.

4. To protect a cast from breaking, pour the plaster to a depth of two or more inches. You can increase the strength of a casting by adding twigs, grasses, or other materials to the uppermost layers of casting medium as it is being poured.

5. Wait twenty to thirty-five minutes, depending on the medium, for the cast to become firm but not completely hardened. Then, gently scratch the date, time, location, and collector's name or initials on the exposed surface of the cast.

6. Allow the cast to fully harden. Remove the dam walls, and use a spatula to loosen the soil around the edges of the cast. With the

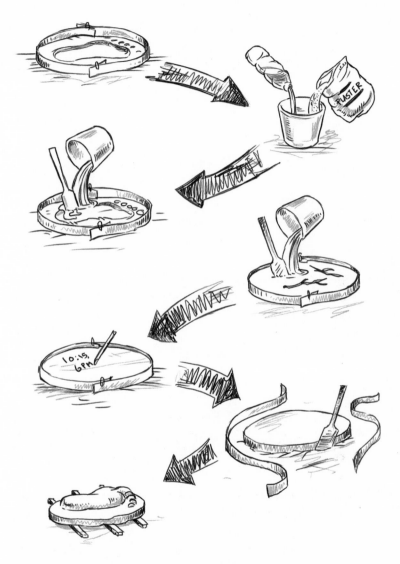

Figure 8. Steps for taking footprint impressions: Practice and patience will pay off with the perfect cast.

fingers of both hands, reach underneath the cast to further loosen it from the soil, then lift carefully. Voila! The cast can be gently washed with a sponge to rid its surface of extraneous dirt. Note: If using plaster, refrain from washing the cast.

7. Place the cast in a safe but well-ventilated place, so the casting medium can continue to cure.

Note: Carrying a large casting kit on longer expeditions on foot may not be feasible. If you find yourself in this situation, Sasquatch scholar Jeff Meldrum recommends bringing a few cans of minimally expanding aerosol foam and several large pieces of cardboard instead. The foam comes in twelve- or sixteen-ounce cans, priced from ten to thirty dollars per can. One can contains enough foam for making impressions of one or two footprints. Spray the foam evenly over a track, placing the cardboard on top as a backing, and then put rocks on top for weight. As the foam hardens, it bonds to the backing, making a detailed model in just a few minutes.

OBTAINING HAIR SAMPLES

If you find Sasquatch hair, by all means save it. But don't make the amateur move of putting that sample in a plastic zip-close bag the way they do on *CSI: Miami* and other police procedurals on TV. The plastic bag will do what it's supposed to do—retain moisture and prevent outside air from seeping in. That may be great for a tuna fish sandwich, but it's not so good for a sample of Sasquatch hair. The plastic bag's food-preserving attributes can also create an ideal environment for mildew, mold, and bacteria to grow. When any of these impurities get into a hair sample, they can confound DNA tests by adding their genetic signatures to the mix.

"The solution is simple," says Scott Moody, an associate professor of evolutionary and organismic biology at Ohio University in Athens. I met Moody online and found him to be a veritable font of practical advice.

"Use a paper envelope, just like you'd use to put a letter in the mail." This method, says Moody, will protect the hair from any mechanical damage without letting unwanted moisture build up inside. Plus, you need only a pencil to write on the envelope, adding the evidentiary details and documenting the chain of custody for this item.

Moody also cautions sample collectors from picking up hair with their hands. "Now you're introducing your own DNA and whatever bacteria is being carried by your hands." It's much smarter to use tweezers, he says. "A few flakes of your skin is all it takes to wreck a good sample," he says.

DNA testing is extremely expensive. That study of thirty hair samples, described in Yikes! The Yeti in Part I, is said to have cost about forty thousand dollars—a price that was paid, in a moment of magnanimity, by the study's principal researcher, Bryan Sykes of Oxford University. Testing a single sample of hair can run up bills in the thousands. Even then, these tests results can only tell if a sample is from an animal other than a Sasquatch; that is, it can provide a negative but not a positive result. That's because we don't know the sequence of genes in the Sasquatch's DNA, and we lack a universally accepted sample on which to base a comparison. Until such a reference can be discovered, a hair sample from a possible Sasquatch can, at best, be classified as an anomalous primate—an unknown.

We know the DNA sequence for a Neanderthal, so it's relatively simple to detect DNA from one. "I'm 2.9 percent Neanderthal," offers Moody, who had his DNA analyzed in 2008 to establish his ancestry. Without the support of DNA tests, it is difficult though not impossible to identify a Sasquatch hair sample. Using a microscope to look closely at its structure and pigmentation, a skilled hair specialist can establish a hair's species of origin. For an expert, it's easier than you'd think to tell a sample of animal hair from that from a human. Our hairs are generally consistent in color and pigmentation throughout the length of the hair shaft, while animal hairs may change color radically over a short distance—a phenomenon called banding. The roots of our hair are usually club-shaped, while the roots of animal hairs are highly variable. The shape of the hair shaft is also more variable in animal hairs. If this sounds confusing, it's because it is—a strong argument for seeking a spe-

THE PANGBOCHE HAND

Without question, DNA testing has become an invaluable ally for determining what is authentic and what is not. It recently solved a key mystery that had puzzled hominologists for the better part of a decade.

In 1958, British explorer Peter Byrne was searching for evidence of the yeti, in the high Himalaya range. While camping at the Pangboche monastery in Nepal, he learned that among the many sacred Buddhist relics was the desiccated hand of a yeti. The monks of Pangboche allowed Byrne to view the hand. However, they denied his request to borrow it for scientific study. They warned Byrne, so the story goes, that various calamities would befall the monastery if the hand were removed.

The following year, Byrne returned to Pangboche with a team of American explorers, intent on collecting some bones from the hand. In secrecy, he removed one of the fingers from the yeti hand, substituting it with the finger bones of a human. The yeti finger was then smuggled out of Nepal and into India, where Hollywood star Jimmy Stewart and his wife, Gloria, agreed to carry it to London—in Gloria's lingerie case, no less.

Upon arrival, the three-and-a-half-inch-long finger was given to W. C. Osman Hill, a British primatologist, for analysis. Osman

>>>

cialist to make the final determination on whatever it is you put in that envelope and brought home from your outing.

Where should you look for Sasquatch hair? Just about anywhere in the vicinity of a sighting. It seems reasonable that a being of this size and hairiness is likely to leave remnants in the patches of foliage it ambles through. Since these beings are said to conceal themselves behind large trees, it makes sense to closely inspect the trunks for patches caught in the craggy bark. James "Bobo" Fay of *Finding Bigfoot* says Sasquatches use telephone poles as scratching posts, leaving behind shed hair in the process. Trouble is, bears also do that. So do humans after a long day of carrying a backpack.

COLLECTING SCAT

Much can be learned by studying an animal's excrement, a.k.a., feces or scat. From cursory examination of this oft-odoriferous evidence, you

<<< Hill's determinations were somewhat ambivalent. Although he initially concluded that the bones were human, he later suggested they belonged to a Neanderthal.

Eventually, the finger wound up in London in the collections of the Hunterian Museum, part of the Royal College of Surgeons of England. There the crusty old digit sat, gathering dust until its rediscovery during cataloguing in 2008. The museum's curators allowed a BBC documentary team to take a DNA sample of the finger, which was then analyzed by genetic experts at the Edinburgh Zoo in Scotland. The test results revealed the finger's DNA to be of human, not yeti, origin. "Human was what we were expecting and human is what we got." Rob Ogden, Head of Conservation Science with the Royal Zoological Society of Scotland, told *BBC News* in 2011.

can estimate the approximate size of a creature, establish the basics of its diet, and determine its location—where it was when it took its most recent dump.

A closer examination of an animal's fecal matter can reveal the more intimate details. Nutshells, seed husks, insect exoskeletons, bone chips, and other indigestible remnants of past feasts are important clues to its maker's identity. By examining Sasquatch scat, we'd know exactly what sustains it, at least during that season. Conversely, if we know what the Sasquatch eats, we can more readily recognize its scat when we see it.

We could also identify Sasquatch scat by what's been gnawing at its insides. The presence of eggs, larvae, and adult forms of endoparasitic invertebrates—cold-blooded critters such as flukes or tapeworms—can also be used to determine whose feces is whose. These parasites are usually species-specific—in other words, the parasites that commonly live inside our pet dogs are not able to survive inside us. Incidentally, some of these internal pests are large enough to be seen with the naked eye. There are more than a thousand known species of parasitic flatworms, the largest of which is one hundred feet long and makes its home in the bowels of a whale.

In *Sasquatch: Legend Meets Science*, noted Sasquatch scholar Jeff Meldrum tells of a presumed Sasquatch scat sample that contained eggs from a nematode worm of the genus *Trichuris*. Actually, *three* kinds of *Trichuris* eggs were identified, each of a different size gradient. The largest of these were "outside the range of human parasite ova," in the words of Meldrum. However, they were still within the expected size range said to infest various other primates. That unique characteristic probably warranted further study, but the lab examiner for this project chose to pass, citing the samples' advanced state of putrescence as sufficient reason to discontinue his analysis.

Fortunately for the finicky, such up-close and personal searches are not always needed. On the trail of a Sasquatch, it could be enough for us to rule out any feces that were obviously left by something other than whom we seek. For some informative visual images of the scat from Roosevelt elk (*Cervis canadensis*), brown bear, or other large animals, read Jim Halfpenny's *A Field Guide to Mammal Tracking in North America*. The kinds of food a creature has eaten can also be inferred by the overall color of scat. Bear feces, for instance, can be brown, black, or bluish in hue. These colors tell us at a glance whether an individual has been dining primarily on pine nuts, raw meat, or berries, respectively.

Final study and species corroboration of scat samples are extremely difficult and, therefore, best left to trained pathologists with access to laboratory facilities. Because of this, any suspected Sasquatch scat should be carefully collected (while wearing rubber gloves) and transferred to a nonreactive plastic container. The sample can then be fully immersed in ethanol and the container tightly sealed to prevent leakage and contamination. If a source of ethanol is unavailable, 180-proof spirits such as vodka or whisky will also prevent samples from deteriorating. As always, include the essential information—date, time, place, and so on—on each evidence tag accompanying the jarred samples.

INTERVIEWING EYEWITNESSES

Photos and audio recordings can be undetectably altered in this, the digital, age. However, eyewitness testimony is not nearly as easy to fiddle with. That may seem improbable—after all, it's nothing more than what someone said they saw. But if their stories are gathered and presented in the form of an affidavit—a written statement that is signed by a person who promises that the information is true—there can be almost no question of its tamper-free nature.

With this in mind, any observations made by team members, or other parties with oral statements to make, should be faithfully taken down in writing. On completion of this task, the eyewitness must be asked to sign their statement on the dotted line. The standard language that precedes the signature goes like this: "I, the undersigned, attest that the information on this page (or pages) is true." This statement should be dated as well and initialed by the signer.

That's it? Not exactly. It also pays to have someone witness the act of signing the document. Ideally, this person should be a notary—most banks and currency exchanges offer notary services free of charge or for a small fee. However, any individual who is willing to swear under oath that they watched as the eyewitness signed the affidavit will do. Once the affidavit is signed, it should be photocopied and stored in a secure place.

To get the facts on paper prior to signing, either interview the eyewitnesses and transcribe what they say or have the witnesses write the statements themselves, describing the events as they occurred. Regardless of method, be sure to have the eyewitnesses give their full name, age, and mailing address. You may need to gently guide the conversation to ensure that all the key points are covered and that testimony doesn't wander off topic. At the same time, take care to avoid putting words in the eyewitnesses' mouth. A skilled interviewer can orchestrate without intruding—a delicate dance with the eyewitness that can require considerable practice to perfect.

Even when you take these steps, there is really no way to evaluate whether the eyewitness experienced what he or she maintains. The field of cryptozoology is rife with false sightings and mistaken claims. It's not necessarily the case that the eyewitnesses were lying. In the heat of the moment, they might have thought what they saw was a Sasquatch or an equally unsettling being.

Take the case of two grouse hunters in Sequim, Washington. In September 1965, they saw what they believed to be a monster coming out

TIPS FOR CONDUCTING AN EFFECTIVE INTERVIEW

Gathering eyewitness testimony can be challenging. The more you do it, the better you will become at getting the information you seek. Before interviewing a witness, it is essential to gain their trust. These tips will help you gather reliable testimony while assuring your witness that your intentions are earnest and that you have their best interests in mind.

Conduct your interview as soon as possible after a Sasquatch sighting or other relevant incident. The information you obtain before a witness has had time to embellish or self-edit their account is often the most useful.

Choose a setting with few distractions: bright lights, loud noises, or competing activities may interfere with the eyewitness' ability to focus and also serve to distract you.

Explain the interview's purpose and how long the interview is likely to take. Ask whether the eyewitness has any questions before you begin, and answer them with honesty, brevity, and compassion.

Assure that the eyewitness testimony will be kept confidential and that you will seek their permission before sharing their information with anyone other than your project team. If their comments are to be quoted in any internal reports, get their written permission to use them this way.

Tell the eyewitness how to contact you at a later date if they want to add information or ask additional questions. Ask whether you may contact them if you need a follow-up interview.

of the woods at dusk. Their reported sighting started talk of a Sasquatch-like being on the prowl. The rumors swept through Sequim like wildfire. The *Sequim Press* wrote that the sighting "had local children terrorized" and people were advised to stay indoors at night. Mercifully, the hubbub was short-lived. The monster was soon located and, upon closer examination, turned out to be nothing more than a weather-beaten, somewhat charred tree trunk.

Can you imagine going public, like the *Sequim Press* did, with a story about a dead tree run amok?

To guard yourself from such embarrassment, any stories, even those signed and sealed, must be regarded as testimony and nothing more. To be accepted as fact, they may need supporting evidence and corroboration by other eyewitnesses.

If this is starting to sound like a legal proceeding, it's because determining authenticity often requires exactly that. Remember *Miracle on 34th Street*? It took a ruling by the New York Supreme Court to establish the existence of Santa Claus in that film.

SHARING YOUR DISCOVERIES

If you've been following the protocols in this book, then you know how complicated it can be to collect original data that will withstand the challenges posed by others with an interest in proving or disproving the existence of the Sasquatch. After several months, perhaps years, in search of the Sasquatch, I suspect you'll feel proud of the information you have obtained. You may also feel protective of your results—after all, you've paid your dues, so why should someone else get the credit for that?

A degree of wariness is a good thing, considering how easy it is for others to take your intellectual property and present it as their own. To safeguard yourself from data piracy, you may choose to keep your research under wraps, at least until you are comfortable with revealing your conclusions to fellow citizen scientists or the public at large.

During the early phases of your Sasquatch-seeking project, such secrecy may be warranted. Yes, there are people out there who aspire to solve the riddle of the Sasquatch by themselves. They may want to do this so badly that they don't care who they steal from or who they slander along their imagined road to fortune and fame.

The existence of these types makes it imperative to choose your friends and allies in your studies with caution. If you've been fortunate enough to find a scientific advisor, he or she may be able to help you publish your findings in a scientific journal or report. By publishing your results, you will establish that your team was the first to address this particular topic— say, a unique feeding strategy or unusual mode of interspecies communication—or shed light on any of the dozens of unresolved questions concerning the Sasquatch's natural history.

As mentioned earlier, your discoveries probably won't get published and shared if you've chosen to work alone. Science is an iterative process, in which the contributions of an individual or team are brought forth to be built upon and enhanced, or altered and occasionally challenged by others in that field. No one person invented the space shuttle or unraveled the complex molecular structure of DNA. On the contrary, these were group achievements that could not have been accomplished by one person operating in a climate of secrecy and suspicion.

Therefore, I encourage you to follow the rules that govern the investigative sciences. As citizen scientists, I urge you to work collaboratively—publishing your hypotheses in scientific papers and posting them on websites, sharing your data with other honest and ethical Sasquatch seekers in the hopes of collectively resolving the mystery of the Sasquatch once and for all.

In this, I wish you the very best of luck.

PART III

HIKING GUIDE

"May your trails be crooked, winding, lonesome, dangerous, leading to the most amazing view." —Edward Abbey, *Desert Solitaire*

LET'S CALL THIS PART GRADUATION DAY. You've learned about the Sasquatch and how to document its existence. It's now time to step outside and start looking for signs of North America's grand enigma in the real world. If you happen to be in the Pacific Northwest, either as a year-round resident or seasonal guest, you've come to the right place. The moderate climate, ample stocks of deer, salmon, and other wild foods and the vast set-asides of wilderness acreage make this part of the world quite hospitable for a large, intelligent, and opportunistic entity such as the subject of this book.

A cursory look at the Bigfoot Field Researchers Organization's state-by-state list of sightings and reports clearly illustrates that, for Sasquatch seekers, this is *the* place to be. Of the more than 4500 sightings and reports in the BFRO database for the United States, more than a third come from the three West Coast states—Washington, Oregon, and California. In Canada, nearly half of all sightings and reports are from British Columbia. At the risk of sounding like a travel agent for cryptotourism, I recommend that people looking for the Sasquatch center their fieldwork in the upper left corner of the continent. Before we explore the places you can wander the woods in search of this elusive being, let's contemplate some of the most well-documented sightings.

NOTEWORTHY SIGHTINGS

NORTHERN CALIFORNIA

❶ In November 1870, the *Butte Record* prints a report of a hairy, five-foot-tall reddish brown wildman that whistled, played with blazing sticks from a campfire, and was later joined by a female of the same species.

❷ The *Humboldt Times* coins the term "Bigfoot" in an August 1958 story describing the discovery of sixteen-inch-long footprints found by a road crew twenty miles north of the Klamath River.

❸ A muddy print of an enormous hand, eleven-and-a-half-inches across, is found in June 1962 on the side of a Fort Bragg home—clearly a sign of a Sasquatch on the prowl.

❹ Roger Patterson and Bob Gimlin put Bluff Creek on the map when they find and film a female Sasquatch *in situ* in October 1967. Over the next two years, dozens of Sasquatch footprints are found and photographed.

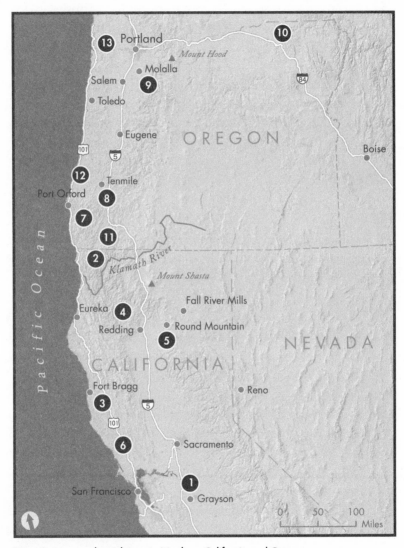

Map 2. Noteworthy sightings in Northern California and Oregon

5 US Forest Service workers find ten-inch-long, ten-inch-wide tracks in deep snow in January 1971. The stride measures five feet, according to the *Klamity Kourier* of Willow Creek.

6 Responding to an alarm call from a ranch near Cloverdale, a law enforcement officer spies a six- to seven-foot-tall being in the headlights of his vehicle in September 2007. This hominid, said to resemble Chewbacca, is covered in thick, matted hair dappled with plant material.

OREGON

7 The seven-foot-tall "Wild Man of the Sixes" is seen three times in one month, according to the *Lane County Leader* in March 1904. The newspaper article also describes his aggressive behaviors—rock throwing and shaking a cabin.

8 In October 1959, two boys reportedly fire guns at a Sasquatch, which tried to chase them away from its territory near Tenmile. Their shots do little to scare away the Sasquatch, which, according to the boys, "screamed like a cat, but louder."

9 Two adults and one juvenile Sasquatch are seen digging holes near a rock pile, presumably looking for ground squirrels to eat, in October 1967. The next year, a Sasquatch is seen stripping leaves from a willow bush and eating them.

10 A US Forest Service patrolman makes casts of Sasquatch footprints in June 1982. The prints have detailed dermal ridges that withstand the scrutiny of forensics experts.

⓫ While hiking with family on the Big Tree Loop Trail of Oregon Caves National Monument in July 2000, a Grants Pass psychologist gets a whiff of a skunklike smell, and, soon thereafter, observes a Sasquatch peering at him from behind a tree.

⓬ After a long day of mushroom hunting near Bandon in October 2004, a man spies a seven-foot-tall Sasquatch-like being covered in reddish blonde hair, running along a two-lane road, clearing it in two bounds, and then hurdling over a four-foot salal hedge on the roadside.

⓭ On a ridge in Tillamook State Forest in July 2013, eyewitnesses report seeing a Sasquatch sitting on a log and then standing up and looking right and left. During a follow-up investigation, a Bigfoot Field Researchers Organization researcher records tapping sounds, possibly produced by the same creature.

WASHINGTON

⓮ In July 1924, prospectors battle Sasquatch-like creatures that attacked their cabin in Ape Canyon, on the slopes of Mount St. Helens.

⓯ The business editor of Portland's daily newspaper, the *Oregon Journal*, claims to have sighted a Sasquatch while driving his car through Satus Pass in July 1963. He has two witnesses (his passengers).

⓰ Local fishermen and others on the Nooksack River delta tell of one or more Sasquatches in the water or on the river's banks—possibly in pursuit of spawning sockeye salmon—from September through December 1967.

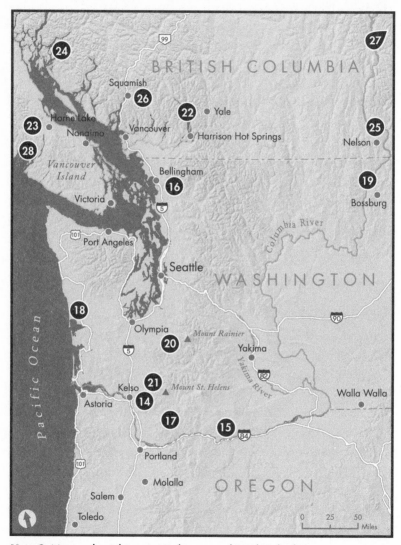

Map 3. Noteworthy sightings in Washington and British Columbia

17 In April 1969, Skamania County passes its now-famous Ordinance 69-01, protecting the Sasquatch from bodily harm.

18 While driving home on July 26, 1969, deputy sheriff Verlin Herrington nearly hits a Sasquatch crossing in front of his patrol car. Framed in the car's spotlight, the Sasquatch walks off the road and into the brush, never to be seen again.

19 Footprints exhibiting a deformity known as *metatarsus adductus* (or skew foot) are discovered near Bossburg in November 1969. A crippled Sasquatch or a clumsy hoax? The experts are divided.

20 Mushroom hunters on a slope of Mount Rainier near the town of National report in September 1990 finding a line of fifteen-inch footprints in a creek bed.

21 The body print of what is presumed to be a male Sasquatch is found in September 2000 pressed into the mud of Skookum Meadows within Gifford Pinchot National Forest.

BRITISH COLUMBIA

22 Later given the name of Jacko, a four-foot-seven ape-man is chased, captured, and incarcerated by a railroad crew near Yale in July 1884.

23 The Victoria *Daily Colonist* describes something strange near Horne Lake in December 1904: a wild man "with long matted hair and a beard, and covered with a profusion of hair all over his body . . . He ran like a deer through the seemingly impenetrable tangle of undergrowth, and pursuit was utterly impossible."

24 A hunter near Toba Inlet says that in the summer of 1924 he was kidnapped in his sleeping bag, carted off, and held captive by a Sasquatch family for several days. Thirty years later, the hunter signs a statutory declaration supporting his oft-quoted claim.

25 Two berry pickers—one human, the other Sasquatch—run into each other north of Nelson in October 1960. The "great beast" is said to be covered with bluish-gray hair, and the human estimated its height at between seven and nine feet, according to the Nelson *Daily News*.

26 In April 1969, workers on a ski development outside Squamish find several miles of fourteen-inch footprints in the snow. Observers suggest the tracks' maker was gathering spruce buds as a food source.

27 Stopping for a snack, an experienced hunter in the Whiteswan Lake area in September 2007 is overcome by a foul odor and, then, discovers the scent's origin—an enormous, upright-postured individual covered in dark brown hair. The hunter reaches for his rifle, but the Sasquatch slips away.

28 From his boat in Clayoquot Sound in February 2014, a young Ahousaht man spots a large creature on the shoreline. As he watches, it stands up from a crouch and heads into the brush. Further investigation uncovers large footprints of two sizes, as well as broken branches and impressions in the ground, suggesting that something big had laid down there. Ahousaht tribal elders discourage others from following the tracks.

The following selection of destinations represents the tip of the iceberg. They are all places with significant records of Sasquatch-human interactions—some historical, others contemporary in nature—making them prime candidates for the focus of your search. While just about any trail in the Northwest could yield significant results, I feel that these hot spots—the Fraser River Valley of British Columbia, the Olympic Peninsula and Mount St. Helens in Washington, Oregon Caves National Monument in Oregon, and Bluff Creek in California—are more likely to satisfy the true Sasquatch seekers among us. I encourage you to add one or two of them to your list of future outdoor adventures.

Last but not least, I encourage you to post the details of your excursions on the Sasquatch Seekers Field Manual website, http://davidgeorgegordon .com/sasquatch/. If you find irrefutable proof of the Sasquatch, I'd like to be among the first to know.

A NOTE ABOUT SAFETY

Safety is an important concern in all outdoor activities. No guidebook can alert you to every hazard or anticipate the limitations of every reader. Therefore, the descriptions of roads, trails, routes, and natural features in this book are not representations that a particular place or excursion will be safe for your party. When you follow any of the routes described in this book, you assume responsibility for your own safety. Under normal conditions, such excursions require the usual attention to traffic, road and trail conditions, weather, terrain, the capabilities of your party, and other factors. Keeping informed on current conditions and exercising common sense are the keys to a safe, enjoyable outing.

—*Mountaineers Books*

FRASER RIVER VALLEY, BRITISH COLUMBIA

"Is it possible that primitive hairy giants still inhabit the mountain solitudes of British Columbia?" John W. Burns asked the readers of the *Wide World Magazine* in 1940. "Scientists and others may scoff at the very idea, but many Indians are sincerely convinced that Sasquatch—or at least a few of them—live to this day in the vast, unexplored interior. And like my Indians [the Chehalis], I also believe."

Nearly a century after Burns shared the Chehalis tribe's legends and introduced their name for the Sasquatch in an issue of *MacLean's* magazine, the Fraser River Valley remains one of the Sasquatch seekers' favored hotspots. In 1938, the Village of Harrison Hot Springs held its first Sasquatch Days festival; after a lengthy hiatus, the event was resurrected in 2012. On occasion, hominologists have gathered at Harrison Hot Springs to swap research findings and mingle with media representatives. An event held there in April 2011 offered a tribute to Sasquatch scholar John Green and featured presentations by noted authorities, including professors John Bindernagel and Jeff Meldrum. Recognizing the importance of their local "wild man," the British Columbia branch of the Chehalis tribe has adopted the image of a Sasquatch as its symbol.

Recently gathered evidence of the Sasquatch's legacy in the Fraser River Valley includes a pair of videos posted on YouTube in 2013, reportedly showing unidentified hominids near Mission, east of Vancouver, British Columbia. The most convincing of the two videos depicts a creature ambling through a wooded landscape, taking enormous strides that appear to be far beyond the physical capabilities of an adult human. CTV News showed the videos to Dr. John Bindernagel, one of Canada's leading Sasquatch experts. Bindernagel expressed some doubts. Nevertheless, CTV noted, the videos had been collectively viewed three hundred thousand times without anyone noticing a zipper or any other clues to suggest a man in a Sasquatch suit.

Of course, it sometimes pays to be skeptical, even after multiple witnesses claim to have seen the same thing. In the mid-1970s, passengers on a bus near Lake Errock, in the Upper Fraser Valley, watched what they later described as an apelike creature darting in front of their vehicle. Attempting to resolve what many people felt was a legitimate Sasquatch sighting, Grant Keddie, curator of archeology at the Royal British Columbia Museum, traveled to Errock, and conducted a thorough analysis of the site.

Keddie was not impressed. "Newspaper reports had described footprints so deep they could only have been made by a creature weighing at least 800 pounds," Richard Watts informed readers of the Victoria *Times Colonist*. "But Keddie said he made deeper prints running in hiking boots."

Further investigation by area police killed what had until then been a lively news story. The police discovered that earlier in the week four men had rented a gorilla suit and then waited at the curbside for a bus to come along—and for the chance for one of them to run across the road.

HICKS LAKE

Distance: 2.5 miles
round-trip
High point: 420 feet
Time: 1½ hours
Agency: Sasquatch
Provincial Park
Map: Park map

Take in a leisurely picnic on a sandy beach along the lakeshore.

How to Get There: East of Chilliwack on the Trans-Canada Highway, turn north (left) on British Columbia Highway 9 (Agassiz–Rosedale Highway). Follow BC 9 north through Agassiz and on to Harrison Hot Springs. Turn right (east) on Lillooet Avenue, and follow it away from the springs. Continue on Rockwell Drive along the southeastern shore of Harrison Lake. When you enter the park, continue on Hicks Lake Road. Stay right at a junction, and then turn right on the access road to the lake.

Trail Description: The 2.5-mile loop runs south from the main Hicks Lake campground around the lake and to the group campground on its northeastern shore. Park in the day-use area and walk through the main campground to the trailhead. About halfway through the hike, bask in the sun on the picnic-perfect sandy lakeshore.

After you've rested, continue on the essentially flat trail. When you reach the group campground, the trail follows the access road back to the day-use parking. If you'd like to look for our elusive creature a while longer in this eponymous park, add on the short trail around the beaver pond north of the lake.

ALOUETTE MOUNTAIN

Distance: 13 miles round-trip
High point: 4480 feet
Time: 10–12 hours
Agency: Golden Ears Provincial Park
Map: Park map

This strenuous trek rewards hikers with a spectacular panorama and virgin stands of mountain hemlock and yellow cedar.

How to Get There: From Lougheed Highway (Highway 7) in Maple Ridge, turn left (north) onto 222nd Street. Go right (east) on Dewdney Trunk Road, and then turn left (north) onto 232nd Street. After you cross the Alouette River, take the first right in the roundabout onto 132nd Avenue, and then almost immediately turn right onto Fern Crescent. At the park's main gate, the road name changes to Golden Ears Parkway. Take the first left onto gravel Mike Lake Road. Look for the Incline Trail near the eastern end of the lake.

Trail Description: This demanding hike climbs 3500 feet in about 6 miles up to the summit of Alouette Mountain. Carry plenty of water in dry weather, and expect snow well into June.

From the shore of Mike Lake, head north on the Incline Trail. Stay left at a junction with the Eric Dunning Trail, which heads back down to Mike Lake Road.

A short while farther at another junction, you can either go left on the Alouette Mountain Fire Access Road or right on the Shortcut Trail. They rejoin. Another Shortcut Trail (less useful than the previous one) branches off to the right—follow either path because they shortly meet back up. >>>

<<< At the next junction, head left up to the summit (the path on the right dead ends). All but this last stretch is open to mountain bikers and equestrians; be aware of and make space for other users.

INDOOR ENTERTAINMENT

Looking for a rainy-day activity to keep your team and yourself occupied indoors? Try holding a Sasquatch Film Festival with a mix of these classics and more contemporary takes on hominology. Arranged chronologically, the following selection of movies aims to entertain and inform. At the very least, you'll learn what *not* to do on your next foray in search of the Sasquatch.

THE SNOW CREATURE (1954)

What could go wrong with a scientific expedition in search of rare plants? Plenty, as evidenced by this low-budget feature, believed to be the first film ever made about the yeti. It's not likely to be on Netflix, so you may have to hunt for this one—but in terms of sheer ludicrousness, it's worth it.

THE ABOMINABLE SNOWMAN OF THE HIMALAYAS (1957)

Filmed in widescreen "Hammerscope," this classic introduced actor Peter Cushing, in the first of his twenty-two Hammer Film Productions appearances, as Dr. John Rollason, a botanist, and Forrest Tucker as his American buddy, Tom Friend. The two men must tussle with the primitive ape-men after Friend's associate, a sharpshooter named Shelley shoots one in cold blood.

>>>

<<<

THE LEGEND OF BOGGY CREEK (1972)

A documentary-style drama set in an Arkansas wetland, where low-brow I-Seen-Ums tussle with something strange. Which of the two is the scariest? You be the judge. The film's style is said to have influenced *The Blair Witch Project* director, Eduardo Sánchez, whose most recent movie, *Exists*, also graces this list.

HARRY AND THE HENDERSONS (1987)

This film's tagline—"When you can't believe your eyes, trust your heart"—conveys the tone of this feel-good fantasy. It begins when a family, returning to their Seattle home after a wilderness outing, strikes a Sasquatch with their station wagon, knocking him out cold. They take him home, and that's when the fun begins. It's "the most popular Bigfoot film of all time," according to cryptozoologist Loren Coleman.

LITTLE BIGFOOT AND LITTLE BIGFOOT 2: THE JOURNEY HOME (BOTH 1997)

These are both family films, free of the violence and gore that shape several other films on this list. Sasquatch is not the villain—the baddies are a logging company in one and a wealthy landowner in the other. The outdoor scenes were filmed in California's San Bernardino National Forest.

SASQUATCH ODYSSEY: THE HUNT FOR BIGFOOT (1999)

Wow—an actual documentary film on this list! This one boasts a cast of cryptozoological luminaries, including noted Sasquatch-ologist Grover Krantz; Robert Michael Pyle, award-winning

>>>

<<< author of *Where Bigfoot Walks*; and Jack Kewaunee Lapseritis, a holistic health educator with a direct line to Sasquatches from outer space.

TENACIOUS D IN THE PICK OF DESTINY (2006)

OK, so there's only one scene with the Sasquatch (played by John C. Reilly), who appears after Jack Black eats some magic mushrooms. Still, it's well worth the wait—about two-thirds of the way through this avant-garde (and frequently off-color) flick.

WILLOW CREEK (2013)

A wobbly, handheld camera's-eye view of what happens when some well-intended Sasquatch seekers travel to the site of the Roger Patterson-Peter Gimlin expedition in hopes of getting some fresh footage. Bobcat Goldthwait, comedian and star of the classic *Shakes the Clown*, directed this one. It's unrated, so expect plenty of gore.

EXISTS (2014)

If you liked *The Blair Witch Project*, you'll love *Exists*. Both movies were directed by Eduardo Sánchez. Instead of a witch, there's Bigfoot, who stalks a group of party hearties through a remote forest in Texas. Viewer discretion is advised, as they say on television.

HOQUIAM, WASHINGTON

With its vast stands of old-growth conifers, near-inaccessible mead-ows, and federally protected wilderness areas, the Olympic Peninsula of Washington represents a haven for Sasquatch searchers. Nearly a million acres of this verdant chunk of land are enclosed in Olympic National Park, officially recognized as a UNESCO Biosphere Reserve and infor-mally branded a Mecca for Sasquatch seekers. Sasquatch encounters from the peninsula account for roughly one-fifth of the Bigfoot Field Researchers Organization's database of reports from Washington State. "Tracks are often found along the Queets River, where some believe Sasquatches are drawn by the large herd of Roosevelt elk," says BFRO's Matt Moneymaker. Nearly half of the reports in his organization's data-base for the peninsula come from Grays Harbor County, on the penin-sula's southwestern edge, where the following story from John Green's *Year of the Sasquatch* is set.

At 2:35 in the morning on Sunday, July 26, 1969, Verlin Herrington, a thirty-year-old deputy sheriff for Grays Harbor County, was driving from Hoquiam to his home in nearby Copalis when he saw a crea-ture on the road. "My first impression was of a large bear, standing in the middle of the road," begins the transcript of Green's tape-recorded interview with Herrington. "I either had to stop for the bear or hit him, so I decided to stop, put on the brakes, came to a screeching halt, and coasted up the slight grade as far as I could without startling the animal."

Whatever Herrington saw that night was erect, very tall, and covered with brownish-black hair. Its face was dark and leathery, with eyes that reflected light. It had humanlike breasts and long muscular legs.

"This animal in my opinion was not a bear, because you could see by the way it was standing that it had no snout . . . I could see in the headlights of my car that it had feet on it instead of paws, and it had breasts," Herrington recalled.

Framed in his patrol car's spotlight, the being—human or beast—walked off the road, down a bank, stopped, and turned, directing its gaze at the off-duty deputy sheriff. Herrington centered his patrol car's spotlight on this strange apparition. He rolled down the window of his vehicle, drew his revolver, aimed it, cocked the hammer, and watched as the creature vanished into the brush.

"I got back in my car and drove off," the rattled police officer added. "Reported the next morning back to the scene and went through the area, found where the animal had gone into the brush and where it had come back onto the roadway."

Herrington found and measured several eighteen-and-a-half-inch footprints. He estimated that whatever crossed his path that night stood between seven and seven and a half feet tall and weighed roughly 300 to 325 pounds.

"It seemed like it took small steps," Herrington told Green. "It was watching me as it walked to the edge of the road. They would be large steps for a human, but for this animal they were short steps. About three steps from the center of the road to the edge."

According to Green, Herrington's superior, the Grays Harbor County sheriff, forbade him to share his incident report with the press. The sheriff issued a statement that the deputy had changed his mind and decided he had seen a bear. "I believe he [the sheriff] simply didn't want dozens of would-be Sasquatch hunters running around on private property in his county and possibly shooting at things, so he took effective steps to prevent it," Green surmised.

JOHNS RIVER STATE WILDLIFE AREA

Distance: 2.5 miles round-trip
High point: 20 feet
Time: 1½ hours
Agency: Johns River State Wildlife Area
Map: USGS 7.5-minute Hoquiam

Stroll through an estuary where you may spot all manner of wildlife, particularly of the winged variety.

How to Get There: From Aberdeen, head west for 11.5 miles on State Route 105. Immediately after you cross the bridge over Johns River, turn left onto Johns River Road. In 0.1 mile, turn left on Game Farm Road. In another 0.1 mile, turn right into the trailhead parking area.

Trail Description: Developed by the Washington Department of Fish and Wildlife, this popular trail offers easy access to this 1500-acre wildlife area. The trail passes through a saltwater estuary teeming with Roosevelt elk and all manner of birds, including herons, grebes, terns, geese, and sandpipers.

LAKE SYLVIA STATE PARK

Distance: Two 2-mile loops
High point: 170 feet (lake loop), 140 feet (creek loop)
Time: 2 hours for both
Agency: Lake Sylvia State Park
Map: USGS 7.5-minute Montesano

Visit a peaceful state park packed with history, natural beauty, and recreation, and enjoy excellent views of mature trees above the lake and creek.

How to Get There: Exit US Highway 12 in Montesano (east of Aberdeen), and head north on Main Street past a traffic light and then scenic county courthouse. Turn left on Spruce Avenue, and three blocks later, turn right on 3rd Street, which becomes Sylvia Lake Road. At the park entrance booth, turn left, cross the bridge, and then park in the day-use area near the ranger's residence.

Trail Description: Two flat, 2-mile loops follow the lakeshore and Sylvia Creek. From the parking lot, head north along the west shore of Lake Sylvia. Cross an old logging road on the northern end, and turn right to follow the lake's eastern shore.

When you emerge in the park's campground, follow its access road back to the booth and across the bridge. Then head south along the lake for a second loop. Cross a cove on an old railroad bridge, and then begin the Sylvia Creek Forestry Trail through City of Montesano City Forest. Keep an eye out for springboard cuts (evidence of logging activity) as you pass through maples and cedars. To close the loop, cross the dam, and return to the parking lot.

FLETCHER CANYON

Distance: 4 miles round-trip

High point: 1450 feet

Time: 2½–3 hours

Agency: Olympic National Forest

Map: Green Trails Mt. Christie No. 166

Explore a remote canyon in the Olympic Mountains.

How to Get There: From Hoquiam, drive north on US Highway 101 for 35 miles. Turn right (east) on South Shore Road, 1 mile south of Amanda Park, and continue on it for 12 miles, passing the Quinault Ranger Station. Look for a small spur road on the south side of the road for the trailhead.

Trail Description: Ignore the trailhead kiosk sign referencing the long abandoned Colonel Bob Trail. Immediately start climbing on a sometimes steep, sometimes rocky route. The numerous side creeks crossing the trail almost guarantee that your feet will get wet.

After gaining a couple hundred feet, the trail rounds a bend and enters deep, dark Fletcher Canyon and soon after, the Colonel Bob Wilderness. Continue climbing under a canopy of hemlocks and firs, while you admire the sword fern–decorated walls. After about 1 mile, the route gets rockier, and the trail approaches Fletcher Creek.

After a slight descent, you break out into a clearing at 2 miles, a good place to turn around. A huge cedar log bridges the creek here, but beyond it, the trail peters out into a tangle of brush.

MOUNT ST. HELENS, WASHINGTON

The slopes of Mount St. Helens, one of the more volatile peaks in the volcanic Cascade Range, have been the site of significant Sasquatch activity, extending back to the earliest days of the European settlement of Washington State. One of the most fascinating of reported encounters appeared in the July 13, 1924, edition of Portland, Oregon's daily newspaper, the *Oregonian*.

The article described how three prospectors, Marion Smith, his son Roy, and son-in-law Fred Beck, plus two companions, Gabe Lefever and John Peterson, had seen tracks and caught glimpses of large, unidentifiable shapes in the region's wilds over the previous six years. These infrequent sightings were without incident, that is, until one of the prospectors decided to fire his rifle as a warning to one of the shapes, telling it in no uncertain terms to stay back.

"I could see the bark fly out from the tree from each of his three shots," Fred Beck recounted in his 1967 book, *I Fought the Apemen of Mount St. Helens*, "Someone may say that that was quite a distance to see the bark fly, but I saw it. The creature I judged to have been about seven feet tall with blackish-brown hair. It disappeared from our view for a short time, but then we saw it, running fast and upright, about two hundred yards down the little canyon. I shot three times before it disappeared from view."

At that point, the ill-defined truce between human and hominid took a turn for the worse. That night, the animals were said to have bombarded the prospectors' pine-log cabin with rocks. These missiles knocked large chunks out of the cabin and one even struck one of the prospectors, rendering the poor chap unconscious.

"The animals were said to have the appearance of huge gorillas," stated the *Oregonian*. "They are covered with long, black hair. Their ears are about four inches long and stick straight up. Their tracks are 13 to 14 inches long. These tracks have been seen by forest rangers and prospectors for years."

According to Beck, the assaults on the prospectors' cabin continued throughout the night. Details of his testimony revealed how the Sasquatches kept pounding in an effort to get in. All the while, the prospectors kept shooting their rifles through the cabin roof, trying to defend themselves from the violent assault. At one point, an arm reached in through the cabin's chinking, nearly snatching an ax away from Marion Smith. In self-defense, Smith fired a round down the ax handle, wounding the creature and causing it to release its grip.

Beck described how one of the miners began singing, "If you leave us alone, we'll leave you alone, and we'll all go home in the morning." He was hoping that the "mountain devils," as the prospector called them, might get the message and go away.

Unnerved, the men finally left the cabin at sunrise, filing their report in the nearby city of Kelso. A search party was dispatched to the scene of the altercation; however, no signs of Sasquatches could be found.

Subsequently, Fred Beck was interviewed numerous times. He stuck to his guns, so to speak, until his death in 1993.

"Did all this really happen?" asks John Green in *Sasquatch: The Apes Among Us.* "I think so. To the people at that time and place, knowing nothing of such creatures except the old legends of mountain devils at Mount St. Helens, the miners' story was not believable. However, if such creatures do exist, then certainly the most acceptable explanation for the miners having claimed to have seen them is that they did see them. There isn't a shadow of suggestion as to why they would make up such a story and keep telling it all their lives."

The area around Kelso continues to be a center of Sasquatch sightings and footprints. The eruption of Mount St. Helens was thought to have leveled the prospectors' cabin in 1980. More recently, though, a team of investigators of paranormal phenomena have claimed they located its remains, buried beneath six feet of debris. The vicinity of the alleged attack on the prospectors is now known as Ape Canyon. That name may have inspired the Mount St. Helens Apes, a local Boy Scout troop whose members discovered and explored Ape Cave—an interconnected series of lava tubes, presumably prime Sasquatch habitat—in the 1950s.

APE CANYON TRAIL

Distance: 9.4 miles round-trip
High point: 4175 feet
Time: 5–6 hours
Agency: Mount St. Helens National Volcanic Monument
Map: Green Trails Mt. St. Helens No. 364

A mile-wide lahar scoured portions of the Muddy River valley, while other parts of the canyon offer features created by eons of erosion from floods and long-forgotten mudflows. The trail visits several small side basins: some are filled with wildflowers and ferns; others are rich woodlands; all are alive with birdsong and critter activity.

How to Get There: From Cougar, drive east on State Route 503, which becomes Forest Road 90. About 1 mile past the Swift Dam, turn left (north) onto FR 83. Drive about 11.8 miles to the trailhead; it will be on the left, about a quarter mile before the road's end at the Lava Canyon Trailhead.

Trail Description: The trail heads alongside the massive mudflow that swept the Muddy River during Mount St. Helens's 1980 eruption. The first mile offers lots of greenery and wildflowers, and then you reach a viewpoint over the lahar basin to the volcano itself. After that rest break, the trail climbs steadily into lush ancient forest. For another 2 miles, you climb through a rich woodland; the massive Douglas-firs are particularly charismatic.

More than 3 miles into your hike, the trail breaks out onto a ridgetop, with views down into Ape Canyon and up onto East Dome on the flank of Mount St. Helens. Turn around at 5.5 miles where you reach the junction with the Loowit Trail just below that dome.

APE CAVE TRAIL

Distance: 2.6 miles round-trip
High point: 2450 feet
Time: 1½–2 hours
Agency: Mount St. Helens National Volcanic Monument
Map: Green Trails Mt. St. Helens No. 364

The primates whose name inspired that of these lava tubes were members of a local Boy Scout troop who found and explored them. They called themselves the Mount St. Helens Apes, and the lava tubes became known as their caves. Note: A powerful flashlight or headlamp with charged batteries is essential for exploring these caves.

How to Get There: From Cougar, drive east on State Route 503, which becomes Forest Road 90 just 1 mile beyond the Swift Dam, and turn left (north) onto FR 83. Drive 2 miles on FR 83, and turn left onto FR 8303. Continue for 1 mile on FR 8303 to the trailhead on the right.

Trail Description: The rough, uneven tubes are long tunnels in thick lava beds that run nearly parallel to the surface of the land. Interpretive signs line both the forest trail and the tubes' entrances. The lower tube is the easiest (but still requires care) and smaller of the two. It is impossible to stay in the caves the entire length between the two entrances. Descending into them requires a jacket—it's a constant, cool 42 degrees down there—and it's dark: bring a flashlight or headlamp.

An enjoyable, level trail through wonderful old forest links these lava tubes and leads from the trailhead to their underworld entrances. At about 1 mile, a small crack allows you to peer into the caves and lets the people inside them see a bit of sunlight. The trail ends at the upper cave entrance.

OREGON CAVES NATIONAL MONUMENT, OREGON

On the outskirts of Grants Pass, Oregon, a local service club called the Oregon Caves Cavemen erected a shrine to their mascot, a club-wielding Neanderthal, in 1972. The statue welcomes visitors to the Oregon Caves National Monument, another hour's drive away. Park your car by the park's visitor center, walk beneath the archway, and step onto the Big Tree Loop Trail. You could find a living example of the Neanderthal's cousin—just like Matthew Johnson, a Grants Pass psychologist, and his family did on July 1, 2000.

"It was around 5:00 p.m. when my family reached this part of the trail," Johnson told Travis Moore, a videographer for the Grants Pass *Daily Courier* in 2008. Johnson and his family were greeted by a tangible sign that something curious was going on.

"Coming downwind through these thick trees and the brush was a very strong stench that smelled as strong as a skunk, but it wasn't a skunk," Johnson explained, reenacting the event for the *Daily Courier*'s video crew. "It had a distinctly different smell but it was something that grabbed your nostrils ... We weren't scared, we just knew there was something up there."

Separating himself from his hiking companions to urinate in the underbrush, Johnson stumbled upon the surprise of his life. "And then out of the left corner of my eye, I saw movement, and I turned and I looked and that's when I saw Bigfoot walk off the pages of myth and legend into reality," he rhapsodized.

Whatever Johnson saw was approximately eight feet tall, human in form but covered with a thick pelt of dark-brown, nearly black, hair. The moment of meeting lasted for a few seconds at best, but to Johnson it seemed like hours. "I was in a major state of panic, not knowing what to do, and, then, had these really protective instincts kick in."

Johnson rapidly advanced toward the Sasquatch, which retreated deeper into the forest, vanishing from sight.

Johnson rounded up his family and walked them briskly back to the trailhead. Returning home, he filed a report, posting it on the Bigfoot Field Researchers Organization website. The BFRO sent Derek Randles, a veteran investigator, to check out the story.

According to the *Daily Courier*, Randles and Johnson suspect that at least two Sasquatch family groups live in the vicinity of the Big Tree Loop Trail. Johnson cofounded the Southern Oregon Bigfoot Society and today, more than a decade after the initial sighting, still leads camping trips to areas around Oregon Caves. While searching the area, he and his cronies have found Sasquatch trails, bedding areas, hand impressions, and footprints that, in at least one instance, led trackers across two miles of terrain. At a bait pile left by the group, Johnson found an ear of corn that, he maintains, had been shucked by a Sasquatch.

LIMPY BOTANICAL INTERPRETIVE LOOP

Distance: 1 mile round-trip
High point: 1300 feet
Time: 30 minutes
Agency: Rogue River–Siskiyou National Forest
Map: National forest map

Interpretive signs describe the relationship of the soil and plants along this easy hike through some of the most notable habitats of southwest Oregon, one of the nation's most biologically diverse areas.

How to Get There: From Grants Pass, take US Highway 199 (Redwood Highway) west of town. Immediately after you cross the Applegate River, turn right onto Riverbanks Road. Follow it 4.5 miles to Forest Road 2800 (Limpy Creek Road), and turn left onto FR 2800-018. Proceed 2.3 miles to the trailhead.

Trail Description: This easy 1-mile loop travels through a variety of forest habitats typical of southwest Oregon and the Rogue River–Siskiyou National Forest. The interpretive signs describe serpentine environments as well as the other special habitats that set this region apart. Relax in privacy along the creek, near a waterfall, or overlooking Limpy Canyon.

BRIGGS CREEK TRAIL

Distance: 9.5 miles point-to-point
High point: 2200 feet
Time: 5 hours
Agency: Rogue River– Siskiyou National Forest
Map: National forest map

Many Oregonians still work claims in this area rich with mining history. This trip is best tackled in late summer or early fall when the creek's lower level makes for easier crossings.

How to Get There: From Grants Pass, take Interstate 5 to exit 61 for Merlin. Drive west on Merlin–Galice Road for about 12 miles to Forest Road 25 (Taylor Creek Road), and turn left. Proceed about 13 miles to FR 2512, and turn right. Proceed a half mile to Sam Brown Campground on the left side of the road. Turn right immediately before the campground fee station to reach the trailhead. You can either hike straight through to a forest road that connects to Selma or turn around when you'd prefer.

Trail Description: This trek on Trail 1132 passes through meadows with promising wildlife-viewing opportunities, and while you must ford it several times, Briggs Creek has delightful, isolated swimming holes. The trail enters a former mining area around mile 4.3, where you cross Briggs Creek. Climb above the creek and back down to Courier Mine to cross the creek once more. There is a nice campsite with a fire ring at 4.9 miles. The trail travels through some old harvest units and some old-growth stands.

The trail's namesake, George E. Briggs, was a packer who supplied early miners in the area. Your hike ends at Soldier Creek near Forest Road 4105-152, which is also accessible from Selma.

WATERS CREEK TRAIL

Distance: 2.5 miles round-trip
High point: 1400 feet
Time: 1½–2 hours
Agency: Rogue River–Siskiyou National Forest
Map: National forest map

Meander on this easy two-loop forested trek year-round.

How to Get There: From Grants Pass, take US Highway 199 (Redwood Highway) west 13 miles to the town of Wonder. Just south of town, turn right (north) onto Waters Creek Road (Forest Road 2200). Travel approximately 2 miles, immediately past the Forest Service boundary, to the trailhead.

Trail Description: This path (Trail 1139) is made up of two connected mile-long loops. Both follow Water Creek with many views of drainages, wildflowers (in season), and frequent animal sightings. They feature hardwoods and conifers, including some scattered old-growth trees, as well as inviting benches and interpretive signs.

SASQUATCH IN POP CULTURE

Although the Sasquatch has been difficult to find in the flesh, its depictions are everywhere. This charismatic figure is prominently featured in novels, short stories, paintings, drawings, music recordings, animated cartoons, chainsaw art carvings, knickknacks—you name it. Even hip-hop artist Ice Cube (hardly a name associated with outdoor exploration) has dedicated his track "Sasquatch" to the big hairy beast.

>>>

<<<   Perhaps the earliest artistic portrayal of Sasquatch appeared, of all places, on the label to a crate of California Giant lettuce. Such labels were originally designed to catch the eyes of fruit wholesalers and distributors, says Loren Coleman, who happened upon this particular design in 2000, while searching for evidence of pre-1958 Bigfoot sightings in California.

"The image on the California Giant brand lettuce fruit label definitely shows a large hairy hominid form," Coleman wrote in his book *Bigfoot! The True Story of Apes in America*. "The figure looks strong, well muscled, with brown, short hair all over the body but on the face. The neck is unusually solid looking and well defined. It is a rather typical image of Bigfoot."

Coleman dates this label to the 1930s or 1940s. He estimates that the model for the Bigfoot-like figure on the label would stand about ten feet tall in real life—certainly within the height range for the Sasquatches in many eyewitness reports.

More contemporary portraits of the Sasquatch tend to mimic the posture and overall appearance of the "star" of the famous Patterson-Gimlin film footage, taken at Bluff Creek. Others have chosen to show an entirely different beast. Seattle painter and muralist Ryan Henry Ward (better known to his fans as Henry) has featured Sasquatches in his large-scale works and on posters for—you guessed it—the aptly named Sasquatch Music Festival, a gargantuan concert series held each summer at the Gorge Amphitheatre in George, Washington. Ward says George Hayduke—the fictional environmental warrior in a pair of Edward Abbey novels, *The Monkey Wrench Gang* and *Hayduke Lives!*—inspires his furry figures.

"I grew up close to the woods and spent lots of time hiking and camping, always wondering if he was out there," says Ward.

>>>

<<< "Then I imagined that, if he was in those woods, he would resemble a member of the Earth First movement, disassembling the industrial nature-mutilating machine."

There are BigFoot Java stands in Bellingham, Tacoma, and Marysville, Washington, and a chain of Yeti Yogurt shops in Seattle, Black Diamond, and Sumner, Washington, as well as Burnaby, British Columbia. You can get a burger and a buzz at Sasquatch Brewing Company in Portland, Oregon, or a cotton "Gone Squatchin'" T-shirt online.

But if you're seeking a trove of Sasquatch-abilia, drop by Archie McPhee in Seattle's Wallingford neighborhood or visit them online. This supplier of toys, gifts, candy, and novelties carries everything from action figures and tiki mugs to plastic bandages, luggage tags, and automobile air fresheners all bearing the image of Bigfoot or Sasquatch in full stride.

You may wonder why the store put so much energy into creating its line of Sasquatch merchandise. "Bigfoot came to me in a dream," says Mark Pahlow, the company's founder and CEO. "He was huge, hairy and smelled like corn chips and dirt. He cupped me in his giant hands and gently lifted me up so that he could whisper in my ear. 'Mark,' he said, 'I came into your dream to give you a word of advice. Take time to read great books, enjoy good food and feed the ducks. Also, if you produce Bigfoot merchandise, you'll make a ton of bread, man.' When I woke up, there was a pinecone on my pillow."

BLUFF CREEK, CALIFORNIA

On an autumn day in 1967, two men on horseback rounded the bend of a Northern California creek and came face-to-face with a Sasquatch. The film footage they captured at Bluff Creek has become the best known, and possibly the most extensively studied, visual evidence of the Sasquatch's existence in cryptozoological history.

Bluff Creek is number one on Loren Coleman's list of Twenty Best Places to See Bigfoot. While you're there, visit the Bigfoot wing of the Willow Creek–China Flat Museum in Willow Creek, Coleman suggests. See the eight-foot-tall Bigfoot sculpture by Jim McClarin or the one at the Legend of Bigfoot museum and shop in Garberville, which, like Bluff Creek, is also in Humboldt County. Willow Creek's annual Bigfoot Days celebration takes place over Labor Day weekend.

In 1967, Roger Patterson and Bob Gimlin, both experienced Sasquatch searchers from Eastern Washington, decided to focus their search on the Bluff Creek drainage. It was a remote, forested site where hundreds of large hominid footprints had been found, some in creek beds miles from any logging roads or human habitation.

The two had been on the trail for a few days when, in the early afternoon of October 20, they suddenly encountered the maker of some of these prints—what appeared to be a female Sasquatch (they called it a Bigfoot), squatting on a sandbar beside the trickling creek.

Although the Sasquatch stayed calm at the sight of the searchers, their horses did not. Reacting to the sight and, presumably, the scent of this unfamiliar being, they reared abruptly. Patterson's horse slipped on the cobbled streambed, landing on its side and dumping its rider in the process. Without a moment's hesitation, Patterson raced after his discovery on foot, simultaneously recording its progress with a rented 16-millimeter movie camera. Gimlin chose to stay behind, calming the horses.

The excited filmmaker drew within about eighty feet of the Sasquatch, whose form then became obscured by the trunks of large trees. More footage was taken as the Sasquatch emerged from the trees, but by then it was considerably farther away. Patterson eventually lost sight of his find in the thick forest understory.

Patterson dropped off the film with his brother-in-law in Yakima, Washington, who took it to Seattle for processing. These twenty-four feet of slightly underexposed, somewhat hazy film, especially the familiar Frame 352, which shows the Bluff Creek beast in three-quarters profile, are now iconic to Sasquatch seekers (this one image now appears on coffee mugs, T-shirts, bumper stickers, and even the logo for a frozen yogurt franchise). The sequence ends, to quote anthropologist John Napier's book *Bigfoot: The Yeti and Sasquatch in Myth and Reality,* "for all the world like a classic Charlie Chaplin fade-out," as the Sasquatch walks out of the camera's view and into the alders, vine maples, and—caution, hikers—poison oak of Bluff Creek.

Now it's your turn to find the film star.

BURNT RANCH FALLS

Distance: 1.5 miles round-trip
High point: 400 feet
Time: 1 hour
Agency: Shasta–Trinity National Forest
Map: National forest map

This relaxing stroll near the Trinity River leads to a pleasant waterfall.

How to Get There: From Willow Creek (east of Arcata), home of the Willow Creek–China Flat Museum featuring the popular Bigfoot exhibit, drive about 15.5 miles east on CA State Route 299. About 0.5 mile before Burnt Ranch, near the turnoff for Hennessy Road, look for the Burnt Ranch campground on the left (east) side of the highway.

Trail Description: Best in fall when you may spy salmon and steelhead trout migrating across the falls, this trail is an easy jaunt. Head downhill from the trailhead 0.75 mile to the river. Take in the rocky, 10-foot wide waterfall as long as you like, and then when you're ready, return the way you came.

BLUFF CREEK BLUNDERS

Critics of the controversial Patterson-Gimlin footage of what appears to be a female Sasquatch, or Bigfoot, on the run offer many compelling arguments against the film's validity. At least three of these pertain directly to citizen science or, more specifically, to the lack of care in handling of what otherwise might have been the firmest proof of this creature's existence.

The first of these arguments revolves around the speed at which the film was taken. For his trip to Bluff Creek, Patterson rented a 16-millimeter camera, which is capable of shooting at speeds of 16, 24, 32, 48, and 64 frames per second. Patterson is said to have routinely filmed at 24 frames per second; however, in his haste to capture his quarry's image on film, he did not note the camera's setting. As a result, viewers of the famous film are hard-pressed to determine whether the Sasquatch was walking, running, or shuffling at a leisurely pace.

Primatologist John Napier claimed, "If the movie was filmed at 24 frames per second, then the creature's walk cannot be distinguished from a normal human walk. If it was filmed at 16 or 18 frames per second, there are a number of important respects in which it is quite unlike man's gait." Had Patterson or his companion Bob Gimlin taken the time to record the camera's speed, scientists might more easily determine whether this being was genuine or merely a man in a monkey suit.

A second challenge is based on the film's altered state. What Patterson put forth as evidence is but a snippet of a much lengthier piece of film. Fully intact, the original film (which, sadly, no

>>>

157

<<< longer exists) would have begun with a leader—an image-free strip of film stamped with the date when it was developed. Without this celluloid strip, it is impossible to verify that the film was shot and developed on the days Patterson claimed it was. The original film would also have contained outtakes—that is, filmed sequences of events that occurred before or after the now-famous encounter. Skeptics suggest that it also might have included alternate takes, demonstrating that the selected sequence was indeed a fake. The lack of these materials casts a shadow of doubt on the brief footage that was submitted as proof.

Last but not least, neither Patterson nor his brother-in-law, Al DeAtley, kept any chain-of-custody records for the film. Nor were they able to establish where the film was developed (DeAtley has stated that this important detail slipped his mind). For this reason, it is impossible to confirm that the key piece of evidence was not tampered with. One is put in the position of taking Patterson at his word.

The following final details are also the thorniest. During his lifetime, Patterson revealed many character flaws. He sold exclusive rights to his footage to several individuals and made a number of extravagant claims that could not be substantiated. The store that rented the camera to him wound up filing charges for theft before Patterson finally surrendered the Cine-Kodak. Several lawsuits were also filed by investors desirous of getting their fair shares of the profits. Would you buy a used Sasquatch—or even a story about one—from this man?

HORSE RIDGE TRAIL TO MILL CREEK LAKES

Distance: 12 miles round-trip
High point: 6000 feet
Time: 6–7 hours
Agency: Six Rivers National Forest
Map: National forest map

The Horse Ridge National Recreation Trail runs north–south about 13 miles through Six Rivers National Forest, the least explored western section of the Trinity Alps. Tackle a section of it so that you may enjoy it in a day. Bring plenty of water on this dry hike.

How to Get There: From Arcata, go east on CA State Route 299 to Willow Creek. Turn north on SR 96, and drive 12 miles into Hoopa Valley Indian Reservation to Big Hill Road. Turn right (east) on Big Hill Road, and drive 11 miles to the national forest border (the road becomes Forest Road 8N01). Continue for 4.5 miles (it becomes FR 10N02) to the Red Cap trailhead. After you leave the reservation, stay on the chip-seal road.

Trail Description: This hike offers gradual ascents and descents along Horse Ridge Trail. Follow the trail 6 miles to Mill Creek Lakes. This very old route turned recreation trail was once used as a supply road between the region's coast and inland settlements.

RESOURCES

SUGGESTIONS FOR ADDITIONAL READING

Blackburn, Lyle. *The Beast of Boggy Creek: The True Story of the Fouke Monster*. New York: Anomalist Books, 2012.

Bord, Janet, and Colin Bord. *Bigfoot Casebook Updated: Sightings and Encounters from 1818 to 2004*. New York: Stackpole, 2006.

Brockenbrough, Martha. *Finding Bigfoot: Everything You Need to Know*. New York: Feiwel and Friends, 2013.

Coleman, David. *The Bigfoot Filmography: Fictional and Documentary Appearances in Film and Television*. Jefferson, NC: McFarland & Co., 2012.

Coleman, Loren. *Bigfoot! The True Story of Apes in America*. New York: Paraview Pocket Books, 2003.

———. *Mysterious America: The Ultimate Guide to the Nation's Weirdest Wonders, Strangest Spots, and Creepiest Creatures*. New York: Simon & Schuster, 2007.

Coleman, Loren, and Patrick Huyghe. *The Field Guide to Bigfoot and Other Mystery Primates*. New York: Anomalist Books, 2006.

Hall, Mark, and Loren Coleman. *True Giants: Is Gigantopithecus Still Alive?* New York: Anomalist Books, 2010.

Healy, Tony, and Paul Cropper. *The Yowie: In Search of Australia's Bigfoot.* New York: Anomalist Books, 2006.

Hunter, Don, with René Dahinden. *Sasquatch/Bigfoot: The Search for North America's Incredible Creature.* Richmond Hill, ON: Firefly Books, Ltd., 1993.

Krantz, Grover. *Big Footprints: A Scientific Inquiry into the Reality of Sasquatch.* Boulder: Johnson Printing Company, 1992.

Markotic, Vladimir, and Grover Krantz. *The Sasquatch and Other Unknown Hominoids.* Calgary: University of Calgary, 1984.

Meldrum, Jeff. *Sasquatch: Legend Meets Science.* New York: Forge Books, 2007.

Morgan, Robert W. *Bigfoot Observer's Field Manual.* Enumclaw, WA: Pine Winds Press, 2008.

Moskowitz Strain, Kathy. *Giants, Cannibals & Monsters: Bigfoot in Native Culture.* Surrey, BC: Hancock House Publishers Ltd., 2008.

Napier, John. *Bigfoot: The Yeti and Sasquatch in Myth and Reality.* New York: E. P. Dutton & Co. Inc., 1973.

Patterson, Roger. *Do Abominable Snowmen of North America Really Exist?* Yakima, WA: Franklin Press, 1966.

Pyle, Robert. *Where Bigfoot Walks.* New York: Houghton Mifflin Company, 1995.

Sanderson, Ivan T. *Abominable Snowmen: Legend Come to Life.* Philadelphia: Chilton Company, 1961; new introduction, New York: Cosimo Classics, 2008.

Shackley, Myra. *Still Living? Yeti, Sasquatch, and the Neanderthal Enigma.* New York: W. W. Norton & Co. Inc., 1986.

ONLINE DATABASES

BIGFOOT FIELD RESEARCHERS ORGANIZATION
www.bfro.net
The oldest and largest organization of its kind; contains the largest database of Sasquatch (Bigfoot) sightings in North America

CRYPTOZOONEWS
www.cryptozoonews.com
Loren Coleman's online blog of cryptozoological news, including Sasquatch sightings and information

NORTH AMERICAN BIGFOOT SEARCH
www.nabigfootsearch.com
Home of the Hoopa Project, an exhaustive examination to establish the optimum location to research Bigfoot, and other topics of scientific interest

THE OLYMPIC PROJECT
www.olympicproject.com/id18.html
"Research with a purpose"—documenting the existence of Sasquatch through science and education

OREGON BIGFOOT
www.oregonbigfoot.com
A subscription service with news of recent sightings as well as an online collection of reports, photos, and recordings of Sasquatch encounters

SASQUATCH INFORMATION SOCIETY
www.bigfootinfo.org
Members-only accessible database and selection of moderated discussion forums about Sasquatch

SASQUATCH RESEARCH
www.sasquatchresearch.net
Sasquatch searcher Jason Valenti's compendium of information about North America's mystery beast; based in Bellingham, Washington

SASQUATCH SEEKER'S FIELD MANUAL
http://davidgeorgegordon.com/sasquatch/
The author's own compendium of anecdotes and information about citizen science and the Sasquatch

SASQUATCH MUSEUMS

CAPRITAURUS BIGFOOT DISCOVERY MUSEUM
5497 Highway 9
Felton, CA 95018
(831) 335-4478
http://bigfootdiscoveryproject.com/

INTERNATIONAL CRYPTOZOOLOGY MUSEUM
11 Avon Street
Portland, ME 04101
http://cryptozoologymuseum.com/

WILLOW CREEK–CHINA FLAT MUSEUM
38949 CA Highway 299
Willow Creek, CA 95573
(530) 629-2653
http://bigfootcountry.net/

FAIRS AND FESTIVALS

BIGFOOT BASH & BOUNTY
Home Valley Park
50092 Highway 14
Home Valley, WA 98648
Contact: Skamania County Chamber of Commerce
(800) 989-9178
www.skamania.org

BIGFOOT DAYS PARADE AND FESTIVAL
Labor Day Weekend
Downtown Willow Creek, CA
Contact: Willow Creek Chamber of Commerce
(800) 628-5156
info@willowcreekchamber.com

OHIO BIGFOOT CONFERENCE
Salt Fork Lodge and Conference Center
Cambridge, Ohio
Annually in May
www.ohiobigfootconference.com/

THE ORIGINAL TEXAS BIGFOOT CONFERENCE

Texas Bigfoot Research Center
Jefferson, Texas
Annually in October or November

SASQUATCH DAYS

Harrison Beach
Harrison Hot Springs, BC
Annually in June
Contact: Tourism Harrison
(604) 796-5581
www.tourismharrison.com/Sasquatch-Days

SASQUATCH SUMMIT

Quinault Beach Resort and Casino
78 State Route 115
Ocean Shores, WA
Annually in November
http://sasquatchsummit.com/

NOTES

INDEX

ABOUT THE AUTHOR

Chona Kasinger

DAVID GEORGE GORDON is the award-wining author of twenty books about nature and the environment. He has written about everything from elephants, orcas, and gray whales to slugs, tarantula spiders, and cockroaches. He's been featured in the *New York Times*, the *Wall Street Journal*, *Time* magazine, *Reader's Digest*, *National Geographic Kids*, and *USA Today*. "Whatever else you say about him, this man is truly a champion of the obscure," observed Japan's *Sinra* magazine. Gordon lives in Seattle with his wife, Karen Luke Fildes, and a tank of tropical fish.

MOUNTAINEERS BOOKS is a leading publisher of mountaineering literature and guides—including our flagship title, *Mountaineering: The Freedom of the Hills*—as well as adventure narratives, natural history, and general outdoor recreation. Through our two imprints, Skipstone and Braided River, we also publish titles on sustainability and conservation. We are committed to supporting the environmental and educational goals of our organization by providing expert information on human-powered adventure, sustainable practices at home and on the trail, and preservation of wilderness.

The Mountaineers, founded in 1906, is a 501(c)(3) nonprofit outdoor activity and conservation organization whose mission is "to explore, study, preserve, and enjoy the natural beauty of the outdoors." One of the largest such organizations in the United States, it sponsors classes and year-round outdoor activities throughout the Pacific Northwest, including climbing, hiking, backcountry skiing, snowshoeing, bicycling, camping, paddling, and more. The Mountaineers also supports its mission through its publishing division, Mountaineers Books, and promotes environmental education and citizen engagement. For more information, visit The Mountaineers Program Center, 7700 Sand Point Way NE, Seattle, WA 98115-3996; phone 206-521-6001; www.mountaineers.org; or email info@mountaineers.org.

Our publications are made possible through the generosity of donors and through sales of more than 600 titles on outdoor recreation, sustainable lifestyle, and conservation. To donate, purchase books, or learn more, visit us online:

MOUNTAINEERS BOOKS
1001 SW Klickitat Way, Suite 201 • Seattle, WA 98134
800-553-4453 • mbooks@mountaineersbooks.org • www.mountaineersbooks.org

OTHER TITLES YOU MIGHT ENJOY FROM MOUNTAINEERS BOOKS

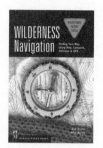

Wilderness Navigation, Third Edition
Bob Burns and Mike Burns
This best-selling text has been updated and reorganized to make it easier to learn this vital skill.

Essential Knots
The International Guild of Knot Tyers
A practical, colorful, and easy-to-use
guide to knots: how to tie them, when
to use them, and why a specific knot is
the perfect choice.

Cairns: Messengers in Stone
David B. Williams
Writing messages with rocks—building cairns, to be specific—is a medium that transcends millennia and continues to speak to our imaginations even now.

Don't! Decks
These compact decks of playing cards
tuck easily into your backpack or pocket.
With outdoor safety and survival tips
printed on water-resistant card stock,
they make a great gift.

Live! From Death Valley
John Soennichsen
A compelling narrative about one of the
most mysterious places on Earth

www.mountaineersbooks.org